AF081131

Silicon Dreams

Inside the Mind of Machine Intelligence

Copyright © 2024 by RK Books

All rights reserved.

No part of this publication may be reproduced, distributed, or transmitted in any form or by any means, including photocopying, recording, or other electronic or mechanical methods, without the prior written permission of the publisher, except in the case of brief quotations embodied in critical reviews and certain other noncommercial uses permitted by copyright law.

This book is a work of fiction. Names, characters, places, and incidents are products of the author's imagination or are used fictitiously. Any resemblance to actual events, locales, or persons, living or dead, is entirely coincidental.

Published by|

Table of Cotents

Chapter 1 The Birth of Silicon Minds 1
    The Origins of Artificial Intelligence 2
    Early Pioneers in AI Research 4
    Turing's Legacy: The Turing Test 8
    From Symbolic Logic to Neural Networks 10

Chapter 2 The Evolution of Artificial Intelligence 15
    The Emergence of Expert Systems: A Revolution in AI 19
    Neural Networks Renaissance: The Deep Learning Revolution 23
    Reinforcement Learning: Teaching AI to Learn by Doing 26

Chapter 3 Understanding Neural Networks 31
    Introduction to Neurons and Synapses 32
    Feedforward Neural Networks: Unraveling the Basics 36
    Convolutional Neural Networks (CNNs): Unraveling the Power of Visual Perception 41
    Recurrent Neural Networks (RNNs): Modeling Temporal Dynamics 45

Chapter 4 Machine Learning: From Theory to Practice 50
    Supervised Learning: Training with Labeled Data 51
    Unsupervised Learning: Discovering Hidden Patterns 55
    Reinforcement Learning Algorithms: Navigating the Exploration-Exploitation Trade-off.. 61
    Transfer Learning: Leveraging Knowledge Across Domains 66

Chapter 5 The Ethics of AI: Challenges and Dilemmas 72
    Bias and Fairness in AI Systems: Mitigating Discrimination and Promoting Equity 74

    Privacy Concerns in the Age of Big Data: Safeguarding Personal Information in a Digital World 79

    Autonomous Weapons: The Moral Debate 84

Chapter 6 Natural Language Processing: Deciphering Human Speec 95

    Tokenization and Text Preprocessing: Enhancing Natural Language Processing 96

    Word Embeddings: Capturing Semantic Meaning 100

    Named Entity Recognition (NER): Extracting Meaningful Entities from Text 105

    Sentiment Analysis: Understanding Opinions and Emotions 109

Chapter 7 Computer Vision: Seeing the World Through Pixels 115

    Image Classification Techniques: A Comprehensive Overview 119

    Object Detection and Localization: An In-depth Exploration 124

    Image Segmentation: Understanding Image Composition 129

Chapter 1
The Birth of Silicon Minds

In the annals of human history, the emergence of artificial intelligence marks a profound turning point. "The Birth of Silicon Minds" chronicles this remarkable journey, delving into the origins, evolution, and implications of machine intelligence. As we embark on this exploration, it's essential to reflect on the transformative power encapsulated within the notion of artificial intelligence.

At its core, artificial intelligence (AI) represents humanity's audacious attempt to replicate and even surpass the cognitive faculties of the human mind. From the early conceptualizations of AI by visionaries like Alan Turing to the modern-day advancements in deep learning and neural networks, the quest for creating intelligent machines has been fueled by relentless curiosity and ambition.

"The Birth of Silicon Minds" invites readers to traverse the historical landscape of AI, unraveling the threads of innovation, ingenuity, and occasional setbacks that have defined its trajectory. We will uncover the pivotal moments in AI history, from the foundational theories laid down by pioneers to the groundbreaking applications reshaping industries and societies today.

Moreover, this chapter serves as a prelude to the broader narrative woven throughout the book, offering a foundational understanding of the principles and paradigms underlying artificial intelligence. As we embark on this intellectual odyssey, let us ponder the implications of bestowing the mantle of intelligence upon silicon substrates and contemplate the profound questions that arise from this endeavor.

The Origins of Artificial Intelligence

The quest to create machines that exhibit intelligence traces back to ancient times, where myths and legends often depicted beings endowed with human-like cognitive abilities. However, the formal study of artificial intelligence (AI) as a scientific discipline began to take shape in the mid-20th century, laying the groundwork for the technological revolution that would follow.

The roots of AI can be traced back to the seminal work of mathematician and logician Alan Turing. In his groundbreaking paper "Computing Machinery and Intelligence" published in 1950, Turing proposed a test to determine whether a machine could exhibit intelligent behavior indistinguishable from that of a human. This test, now famously known as the Turing Test, became a cornerstone in the field of AI research, sparking interest and debate among scientists and philosophers alike.

Following Turing's lead, a cohort of pioneering researchers set out to explore the theoretical underpinnings of artificial intelligence. One such luminary was John McCarthy, who is credited with coining the term "artificial intelligence" in 1956. McCarthy, along with fellow researchers Marvin Minsky, Nathaniel Rochester, and Claude Shannon, organized the seminal Dartmouth Conference, which marked the official birth of AI as a field of study.

During the early years of AI research, the prevailing approach centered around symbolic reasoning and logic. This approach, known as "good old-fashioned AI" or symbolic AI, aimed to emulate human intelligence by manipulating symbols and rules according to predefined algorithms. Symbolic AI systems were designed to perform tasks such as problem-solving, theorem proving, and natural language understanding using symbolic representations of knowledge.

One of the earliest success stories in symbolic AI was the creation of expert systems. These systems, developed in the 1970s and 1980s, employed rule-based reasoning to emulate the expertise of human experts in specific domains. Expert systems found applications in areas such as medical diagnosis, financial analysis, and industrial process control, showcasing the potential of AI to automate complex decision-making tasks.

However, the limitations of symbolic AI soon became apparent. Symbolic AI systems struggled to cope with the inherent uncertainty and ambiguity present in real-world data and tasks. Moreover, they often required extensive hand-crafting of rules and knowledge representations, making them brittle and difficult to scale.

In response to these challenges, a paradigm shift occurred in the field of AI with the emergence of connectionism and neural networks. Inspired by the structure and function of the human brain, neural network models sought to simulate the behavior of interconnected neurons to learn and adapt from data. This approach, known as "connectionism," offered a more flexible and data-driven alternative to symbolic AI.

The resurgence of interest in neural networks can be attributed in part to the pioneering work of researchers such as Frank Rosenblatt, who developed the perceptron model in the late 1950s, and later, to the breakthroughs in backpropagation algorithm by Geoffrey Hinton, David Rumelhart, and Ronald Williams in the 1980s. These developments laid the groundwork for the modern era of deep learning, characterized by the training of deep neural networks with multiple layers of abstraction.

The advent of deep learning has led to unprecedented progress in AI across a wide range of applications, including computer vision, natural language processing, and autonomous systems. Deep learning algorithms have achieved human-level performance or surpassed human experts in tasks such as image recognition, speech recognition, and game playing, demonstrating the transformative potential of AI in the digital age.

In conclusion, the origins of artificial intelligence can be traced back to the visionary ideas of pioneers like Alan Turing and John McCarthy, who laid the groundwork for the scientific study of intelligent machines. From the early days of symbolic AI to the current era of deep learning, the field of AI has witnessed remarkable advancements driven by interdisciplinary collaboration, computational innovation, and a relentless pursuit of understanding the nature of intelligence. As we stand on the cusp of the AI revolution, it is essential to reflect on the rich tapestry of ideas and discoveries that have shaped the trajectory of artificial intelligence and to ponder the possibilities and challenges that lie ahead.

Early Pioneers in AI Research

The history of artificial intelligence (AI) is replete with the contributions of visionary thinkers, scientists, and researchers who laid the foundations for the field's development. From the conceptualization of intelligent machines to the formalization of AI as a scientific discipline, these early pioneers played a pivotal role in shaping the trajectory of AI research. In this exploration of the early history of AI, we delve into the lives and contributions of some of the key figures who paved the way for the modern era of artificial intelligence.

1. Alan Turing: The Father of Computer Science

Alan Turing, a British mathematician, logician, and cryptanalyst, is widely regarded as one of the founding fathers of computer science and artificial intelligence. Turing's seminal work laid the groundwork for the theoretical underpinnings of computation and intelligent machines. His groundbreaking paper "Computing Machinery and Intelligence," published in 1950, introduced the concept of the Turing Test—a method for determining whether a machine exhibits intelligent behavior indistinguishable from that of a human.

Turing's theoretical framework provided a blueprint for the development of early AI systems and sparked interest and debate among scientists and philosophers about the nature of intelligence and consciousness. His pioneering contributions to the fields of computability theory, cryptography, and artificial intelligence laid the foundation for the digital revolution that would follow.

2. John McCarthy: The Architect of Artificial Intelligence

John McCarthy, an American computer scientist, is credited with coining the term "artificial intelligence" and organizing the seminal Dartmouth Conference in 1956, which marked the birth of AI as a field of study. McCarthy's vision of AI as a scientific discipline focused on the design and implementation of intelligent systems capable of reasoning, learning, and problem-solving.

Throughout his career, McCarthy made significant contributions to various subfields of AI, including symbolic reasoning, expert systems, and formal logic. He developed the LISP programming language, which became a key tool for AI research and implementation. McCarthy's enduring legacy lies in his role as a pioneering advocate for AI and his efforts to establish it as a legitimate area of scientific inquiry.

3. Herbert Simon and Allen Newell: The Pioneers of Cognitive Science

Herbert Simon and Allen Newell were American computer scientists and cognitive psychologists who made pioneering contributions to the development of artificial intelligence and cognitive science. Together, they developed the Logic Theorist, the first AI program capable of proving mathematical theorems—a feat that demonstrated the potential of computers to emulate human problem-solving abilities.

Simon and Newell's research laid the foundation for the "physical symbol system hypothesis," which posits that any system capable of manipulating symbols according to formal rules could be considered intelligent. Their work paved the way for the development of symbolic AI systems and influenced subsequent approaches to AI research, including expert systems and cognitive modeling.

4. Marvin Minsky: The Father of Neural Networks

Marvin Minsky, an American cognitive scientist and co-founder of the MIT AI Laboratory, made significant contributions to the study of artificial intelligence, robotics, and cognitive psychology. Minsky's research focused on understanding the principles of human cognition and replicating them in artificial systems.

One of Minsky's most influential contributions was the development of the perceptron, an early neural network model capable of learning simple patterns. Although the perceptron had limitations and fell out of favor for a time, Minsky's work laid the foundation for the resurgence of interest in neural networks decades later.

5. Norbert Wiener: The Pioneer of Cybernetics

Norbert Wiener, an American mathematician and philosopher, is often regarded as the father of cybernetics—the interdisciplinary study of control and communication in living organisms and machines. Wiener's groundbreaking book "Cybernetics: Or Control and Communication in the Animal and the Machine," published in 1948, laid the theoretical groundwork for the field of artificial intelligence.

Wiener's ideas about feedback mechanisms, self-regulation, and information processing influenced the development of early AI systems and robotics. His interdisciplinary approach to understanding complex systems paved the way for the integration of cybernetics, neuroscience, and computer science in the study of intelligent behavior.

6. Claude Shannon: The Father of Information Theory

Claude Shannon, an American mathematician, electrical engineer, and cryptographer, made seminal contributions to the field of information theory, which laid the mathematical foundation for modern digital communication and computing systems. Shannon's landmark paper "A Mathematical Theory of Communication," published in 1948, introduced the concept of entropy and established the theoretical framework for understanding communication and information processing.

Shannon's insights into information theory provided essential tools for AI researchers to formalize concepts such as uncertainty, entropy, and information encoding. His work on the mathematical principles of communication influenced the development of early AI algorithms and machine learning techniques.

The early pioneers in AI research laid the foundation for the modern era of artificial intelligence, shaping the trajectory of the field with their visionary ideas, groundbreaking discoveries, and interdisciplinary collaborations. From Alan Turing's conceptualization of intelligent machines to Claude Shannon's mathematical theory of communication, their contributions continue to reverberate in the ongoing quest to understand and replicate intelligent behavior in machines. As we stand on the shoulders of these giants, it is essential to recognize and celebrate their enduring legacy in the annals of scientific history.

Turing's Legacy: The Turing Test

Alan Turing's legacy in the field of artificial intelligence is perhaps most enduringly captured by his proposition of the Turing Test. This iconic concept, introduced in his seminal 1950 paper "Computing Machinery and Intelligence," not only sparked profound philosophical debates but also served as a catalyst for the development of AI research and the quest to create intelligent machines. In this exploration of Turing's legacy and the Turing Test, we delve into the origins of the test, its implications for AI research, and its enduring relevance in the digital age.

1. The Origins of the Turing Test

Alan Turing's fascination with the nature of intelligence and consciousness drove him to ponder the question of whether machines could exhibit human-like intelligence. In his landmark paper, Turing proposed a simple yet profound thought experiment to address this question—the Turing Test. The essence of the test lies in its ability to assess a machine's ability to exhibit intelligent behavior indistinguishable from that of a human.

The Turing Test involves a human evaluator engaging in a natural language conversation with both a human and a machine, without knowing which is which. If the evaluator cannot reliably distinguish between the human and the machine based on the conversation alone, then the machine is said to have passed the Turing Test and demonstrated human-like intelligence.

Turing envisioned the Turing Test not as a definitive measure of machine intelligence but rather as a provocative thought experiment to stimulate philosophical inquiry and scientific exploration. By proposing a practical criterion for assessing machine intelligence,

Turing sought to bridge the gap between abstract philosophical speculation and empirical scientific inquiry.

2. Philosophical Implications of the Turing Test

The Turing Test has profound philosophical implications for our understanding of intelligence, consciousness, and the nature of humanity. By framing the question of machine intelligence in terms of observable behavior rather than inner mental states, Turing challenged traditional philosophical notions of mind and consciousness.

The Turing Test forced philosophers to confront fundamental questions about the nature of intelligence and the possibility of creating machines capable of conscious thought. It sparked debates about the nature of consciousness, the role of language in cognition, and the limits of artificial intelligence.

Moreover, the Turing Test raised ethical and existential concerns about the implications of creating intelligent machines. Turing himself speculated about the potential consequences of AI, including the possibility of machines surpassing human intelligence and the ethical implications of machine consciousness.

3. The Evolution of the Turing Test

Since its inception, the Turing Test has undergone various iterations and adaptations in response to advancements in technology and changes in philosophical perspectives. Early implementations of the Turing Test focused primarily on text-based communication, such as instant messaging or email exchanges.

In recent years, researchers have explored more sophisticated versions of the Turing Test that incorporate multimodal interactions, such as speech recognition, facial expressions, and gesture recognition. These multimodal Turing Tests aim to assess not only linguistic capabilities but also perceptual and social intelligence.

Furthermore, advancements in AI technology have led to the development of chatbots and virtual assistants that claim to pass the Turing Test by engaging in natural language conversations with users. However, critics argue that these systems often rely on clever tricks and pre-programmed responses rather than genuine understanding or intelligence.

4. The Legacy of the Turing Test

Despite ongoing debates and controversies surrounding the Turing Test, its legacy endures as a symbol of the quest for artificial intelligence and the philosophical exploration of the nature of mind and consciousness. The Turing Test continues to inspire AI researchers, philosophers, and ethicists to grapple with fundamental questions about the limits and possibilities of machine intelligence.

Moreover, the Turing Test serves as a touchstone for assessing progress in AI research and development. While no machine has yet passed a stringent version of the Turing Test convincingly, ongoing advancements in natural language processing, machine learning, and cognitive science bring us closer to realizing Turing's vision of creating intelligent machines.

Alan Turing's proposition of the Turing Test represents a pivotal moment in the history of artificial intelligence and philosophical inquiry. By proposing a practical criterion for assessing machine intelligence, Turing sparked debates that continue to resonate in the digital age. As AI technology advances and the quest for machine intelligence continues, the Turing Test remains a beacon guiding our exploration of the frontiers of human knowledge and understanding.

From Symbolic Logic to Neural Networks

The evolution of artificial intelligence (AI) has been marked by a shift in paradigms—from early approaches grounded in symbolic logic and rule-based reasoning to more recent advancements driven by the rise of neural networks and machine learning. In this exploration of the transition from symbolic logic to neural networks, we delve into the historical context, key developments, and implications for the field of AI.

1. The Early Days of Symbolic AI

The early days of AI research, often referred to as the "good old-fashioned AI" or symbolic AI era, were characterized by an emphasis on symbolic reasoning and logic-based approaches. Researchers sought to emulate human intelligence by encoding knowledge and rules of inference into computer programs.

One of the seminal achievements of symbolic AI was the development of expert systems—AI programs designed to emulate the expertise of human experts in specific domains. These systems employed rule-based reasoning to process symbolic representations of knowledge and make inferences based on logical rules.

The success of expert systems in applications such as medical diagnosis, financial analysis, and industrial process control fueled optimism about the potential of symbolic AI to replicate human cognitive abilities. However, the limitations of rule-based approaches became increasingly apparent as AI researchers encountered challenges in dealing with uncertainty, ambiguity, and complexity in real-world tasks.

2. The AI Winter and the Rise of Connectionism

The symbolic AI paradigm began to wane in the 1980s, amidst growing skepticism about its ability to tackle the inherent limitations of complex real-world problems. The period that followed, known as the "AI winter," saw a decline in funding and interest in AI research, as early optimism gave way to disillusionment.

Amidst this backdrop, a new paradigm known as connectionism emerged as an alternative to symbolic AI. Inspired by the structure and function of the human brain, connectionist models sought to simulate the behavior of interconnected neurons to learn and adapt from data.

One of the key developments in connectionism was the resurgence of interest in neural networks—computational models composed of interconnected nodes, or "neurons," organized into layers. Neural networks are capable of learning complex patterns and relationships from data through a process known as "training" or "learning."

3. The Revival of Neural Networks

The revival of neural networks can be attributed in part to the pioneering work of researchers such as Frank Rosenblatt, who developed the perceptron model—a simple neural network capable of learning linearly separable patterns. However, initial enthusiasm for neural networks waned following the publication of the perceptron's limitations in solving non-linearly separable problems.

The breakthroughs in neural network research came in the 1980s with the development of the backpropagation algorithm by Geoffrey Hinton, David Rumelhart, and Ronald Williams. Backpropagation enabled efficient training of multi-layer neural networks, known as "deep" neural networks, which could learn hierarchical representations of data.

The resurgence of interest in neural networks, fueled by advancements in computational power and data availability, led to the development of powerful new architectures such as convolutional neural networks (CNNs) for image recognition and recurrent neural networks (RNNs) for sequence modeling.

4. The Rise of Deep Learnin

The culmination of these advancements in neural network research gave rise to the modern era of deep learning—a subfield of machine learning that focuses on training deep neural networks with multiple layers of abstraction. Deep learning has revolutionized AI research and applications, enabling breakthroughs in areas such as computer vision, natural language processing, and reinforcement learning.

One of the key advantages of deep learning is its ability to automatically learn hierarchical representations of data, capturing complex patterns and relationships without the need for hand-crafted features or rules. This data-driven approach has proven highly effective in domains where large amounts of labeled data are available, such as image and speech recognition.

The success of deep learning has led to widespread adoption across industries and domains, driving innovations in areas such as autonomous vehicles, healthcare, finance, and robotics. Deep learning has also fueled advancements in AI research, pushing the boundaries of what is possible in terms of machine perception, reasoning, and decision-making.

5. Implications and Future Directions

The transition from symbolic AI to neural networks has profound implications for the field of artificial intelligence. While symbolic AI approaches excel in domains where explicit rules and knowledge representations are available, neural networks have demonstrated superior performance in tasks requiring pattern recognition, classification, and prediction.

The integration of symbolic and connectionist approaches represents a promising direction for future research, as researchers seek to develop hybrid AI systems that leverage the strengths of both paradigms. Combining symbolic reasoning with neural network-based learning could enable AI systems to reason and learn from data in a more human-like manner.

Furthermore, ongoing advancements in neural network research, such as the development of attention mechanisms, memory-augmented architectures, and neuro-symbolic approaches, hold the promise of addressing the limitations of current deep learning systems and unlocking new capabilities in AI.

The transition from symbolic logic to neural networks represents a paradigm shift in the field of artificial intelligence, marking a departure from rule-based approaches towards data-driven learning. The resurgence of interest in neural networks and the rise of deep learning have propelled AI research and applications to new heights, paving the way for intelligent systems capable of understanding, reasoning, and learning from the vast amounts of data available in the digital age. As we continue to explore the frontiers of AI, the integration of symbolic and connectionist approaches promises to usher in a new era of human-centered artificial intelligence, with profound implications for society, technology, and the future of humanity.

Chapter 2
The Evolution of Artificial Intelligence

The evolution of artificial intelligence (AI) stands as a testament to humanity's relentless pursuit of understanding and replicating intelligence. "The Evolution of Artificial Intelligence" embarks on a journey through the annals of history, tracing the transformative developments that have shaped the landscape of AI research and applications.

From its humble beginnings as a speculative concept to its current status as a pervasive force in our daily lives, AI has undergone a remarkable evolution driven by a convergence of scientific breakthroughs, technological advancements, and societal changes. As we embark on this exploration, it's essential to appreciate the historical context and pivotal moments that have propelled AI from the realm of science fiction to practical reality.

This chapter serves as a prelude to the broader narrative unfolding throughout the book, offering a panoramic view of the key milestones, trends, and challenges that have defined the evolution of artificial intelligence. From early philosophical inquiries into the nature of mind and intelligence to the emergence of modern AI technologies such as machine learning and deep learning, the story of AI is one of innovation, perseverance, and paradigm shifts.

As we delve into the rich tapestry of AI's evolution, let us reflect on the profound implications of our quest to create intelligent machines and the ethical, societal, and existential questions that arise from this endeavor. Whether viewed through the lens of history, science, or philosophy, the evolution of artificial intelligence remains an extraordinary testament to human ingenuity and imagination, offering glimpses into the boundless potential of our technological future.

AI Winters: Challenges and Resilience

The history of artificial intelligence (AI) is punctuated by periods of fervent enthusiasm followed by periods of disillusionment and stagnation—often referred to as "AI winters." These periods of retrenchment and skepticism have been characterized by dwindling funding, waning interest, and a sense of disillusionment with the promise of AI. In this exploration of AI winters, we delve into the causes, consequences, and resilience of the field in the face of adversity.

1. The First AI Winter (1970s-1980s)

The first AI winter occurred in the 1970s and 1980s, following the initial wave of optimism and excitement surrounding the field of artificial intelligence. During this period, early AI research faced numerous challenges, including limitations in computing power, algorithmic complexity, and the inability of existing AI systems to meet the high expectations set by researchers and policymakers.

One of the contributing factors to the first AI winter was the overpromising and underdelivering of AI technologies, leading to unrealistic expectations and subsequent disappointment when early AI systems failed to live up to the hype. Additionally, funding agencies and policymakers became increasingly skeptical about the feasibility and practicality of AI research, leading to a decline in research funding and support.

Despite these challenges, the first AI winter also laid the groundwork for important advancements in AI research, including the development of expert systems, knowledge-based systems, and symbolic reasoning techniques. While these approaches ultimately fell short of achieving human-level intelligence, they provided valuable insights and methodologies that would later inform the resurgence of interest in AI.

2. The Second AI Winter (Late 1980s-1990s)

The second AI winter occurred in the late 1980s and 1990s, fueled by a combination of factors including technological limitations, economic downturns, and public skepticism about the practical applications of AI. During this period, AI research faced criticism from both within and outside the scientific community, with some critics questioning the fundamental premise of AI as a field of study.

One of the contributing factors to the second AI winter was the failure of early AI systems to scale up to real-world problems and domains beyond the narrow confines of expert systems and rule-based reasoning. Additionally, the economic recession of the early 1990s led to budget cuts and reduced funding for academic research and development, further exacerbating the challenges facing the AI community.

Despite the setbacks of the second AI winter, the period also witnessed important advancements in neural network research, including the development of backpropagation and other learning algorithms. These advancements laid the foundation for the resurgence of interest in AI in the late 1990s and early 2000s, as researchers began to explore new approaches to machine learning and data-driven AI.

3. Resilience and Renewal

Despite the challenges posed by AI winters, the field of artificial intelligence has demonstrated remarkable resilience and adaptability in the face of adversity. Each AI winter has been followed by a period of renewal and resurgence, driven by advancements in technology, changes in societal attitudes, and shifts in research paradigms.

One of the key factors contributing to the resilience of AI has been the exponential growth of computing power and the availability of large-scale datasets, which have enabled breakthroughs in areas such as deep learning, reinforcement learning, and natural language processing. These advancements have fueled the development of AI technologies with unprecedented capabilities, revolutionizing industries and transforming society in profound ways.

Additionally, the increasing integration of AI into everyday life—from virtual assistants and recommendation systems to autonomous vehicles and medical diagnostics—has helped to dispel skepticism and skepticism surrounding the practical applications of AI. As AI becomes increasingly pervasive and indispensable in our daily lives, the barriers to adoption and acceptance continue to diminish, paving the way for continued growth and innovation in the field

Furthermore, the interdisciplinary nature of AI research, spanning computer science, neuroscience, psychology, and other disciplines, has fostered collaboration and cross-pollination of ideas, leading to novel approaches and breakthroughs in AI. As researchers continue to push the boundaries of what is possible in AI, the field remains poised for continued growth and impact in the years to come.

AI winters represent periods of retrenchment and skepticism in the field of artificial intelligence, marked by declining funding, waning interest, and a sense of disillusionment with the promise of AI. However, these periods of adversity have also catalyzed resilience, innovation, and renewal in the AI community, leading to important advancements and breakthroughs that have reshaped the trajectory of the field. As AI continues to evolve and mature, the lessons learned from past AI winters serve as a reminder of the challenges and opportunities inherent in the pursuit of artificial intelligence.

The Emergence of Expert Systems: A Revolution in AI

Expert systems represent a significant milestone in the evolution of artificial intelligence (AI), marking a shift towards practical applications of AI technologies in solving real-world problems. Emerging in the 1970s and reaching their peak in the 1980s, expert systems revolutionized industries, ranging from medicine to finance, by emulating the decision-making capabilities of human experts. In this comprehensive exploration, we delve into the origins, principles, development, applications, and legacy of expert systems, shedding light on their profound impact on AI and society.

1. Origins and Principles of Expert System

Expert systems originated from the intersection of AI, cognitive psychology, and computer science, drawing inspiration from the human cognitive process of problem-solving and decision-making. The fundamental premise of expert systems lies in the encoding of human expertise, knowledge, and reasoning into computer programs, enabling them to emulate the decision-making capabilities of domain experts in specific fields.

At the heart of expert systems are knowledge representations and inference mechanisms that capture and manipulate domain-specific knowledge. Knowledge is typically represented using symbolic languages such as rules, frames, or semantic networks, allowing experts to encode their expertise in a form understandable to computers. Inference mechanisms, such as rule-based reasoning or probabilistic reasoning, enable expert systems to make deductions, draw conclusions, and provide recommendations based on the encoded knowledge.

The development of expert systems was driven by advancements in AI research, including symbolic reasoning, knowledge representation, and problem-solving techniques. Early expert systems, such as Dendral for chemical analysis and MYCIN for medical diagnosis, demonstrated the potential of AI to automate complex decision-making tasks previously reserved for human experts.

2. Development and Evolution of Expert Systems

The development of expert systems can be traced back to pioneering efforts in the 1960s and 1970s, with early systems focusing on narrow domains and simple problem-solving tasks. One of the earliest examples of an expert system is Dendral, developed at Stanford University in the 1960s, which automated the interpretation of mass spectrometry data for chemical analysis.

The 1980s witnessed a surge of interest and investment in expert systems, fueled by advancements in AI research, increased computing power, and the availability of commercial off-the-shelf software tools. Companies and organizations across industries embraced expert systems as a means to enhance productivity, improve decision-making, and reduce reliance on human expertise.

The rise of expert systems also led to the development of specialized software tools and programming languages for building and deploying expert systems, such as CLIPS, OPS5, and PROLOG. These tools provided developers with the necessary infrastructure and methodologies to encode domain knowledge and develop custom-tailored expert systems for specific applications.

3. Applications of Expert Systems

Expert systems found applications in a wide range of domains and industries, including healthcare, finance, engineering, manufacturing, and telecommunications. In healthcare, expert systems such as MYCIN and CADUCEUS were developed to assist physicians in diagnosing diseases and recommending treatment plans based on patient data and medical knowledge.

In finance, expert systems were employed for tasks such as credit scoring, risk assessment, and investment advisory. Systems like XCON, developed by Digital Equipment Corporation, revolutionized the manufacturing industry by automating the configuration of complex products and systems based on customer requirements and engineering constraints.

Other notable applications of expert systems include fault diagnosis in telecommunications networks, route planning in transportation logistics, and quality control in manufacturing processes. Expert systems proved to be invaluable tools for automating routine decision-making tasks, improving efficiency, and reducing errors in various domains.

4. Challenges and Limitations

Despite their widespread adoption and success in certain domains, expert systems faced several challenges and limitations that ultimately contributed to their decline in popularity. One of the primary challenges was the knowledge acquisition bottleneck— the process of eliciting, encoding, and maintaining domain knowledge within expert systems.

Knowledge acquisition often required extensive collaboration between domain experts and knowledge engineers, leading to time-consuming and costly development processes. Additionally, the brittleness of rule-based systems made them susceptible to errors and inaccuracies when faced with novel or ambiguous situations outside their predefined knowledge base.

The interpretability and explainability of expert systems also raised concerns, particularly in critical domains such as healthcare and finance, where transparency and accountability are paramount. Users and stakeholders often demanded explanations for the system's recommendations and decisions, which could be challenging to provide with rule-based systems.

Moreover, the rapid advancement of alternative AI approaches, such as neural networks and machine learning, offered new opportunities for tackling complex problems that were beyond the capabilities of rule-based expert systems. These approaches, which relied on data-driven learning algorithms rather than handcrafted rules, demonstrated superior performance in tasks such as pattern recognition, natural language processing, and decision-making.

5. Legacy and Future Directions

Despite their eventual decline in popularity, the legacy of expert systems lives on in the principles, methodologies, and technologies that continue to shape the field of artificial intelligence. The development of expert systems laid the foundation for subsequent advancements in AI, including knowledge-based systems, decision support systems, and intelligent tutoring systems.

Moreover, the challenges and lessons learned from the era of expert systems have informed ongoing research efforts in areas such as knowledge representation, reasoning under uncertainty, and human-computer interaction. Concepts such as explainable AI and hybrid intelligent systems, which combine rule-based and data-driven approaches, are gaining traction as researchers seek to address the limitations of traditional expert systems.

The emergence of expert systems represented a revolutionary moment in the history of artificial intelligence, marking a transition from speculative theories to practical applications. Despite their eventual decline, expert systems left an indelible mark on the field of AI, shaping its development and influencing subsequent generations of researchers and practitioners. As AI continues to evolve and mature, the principles and methodologies of expert systems remain relevant, serving as a testament to the enduring impact of this transformative era in AI history.

Neural Networks Renaissance: The Deep Learning Revolution

The renaissance of neural networks, often referred to as the deep learning revolution, represents a watershed moment in the field of artificial intelligence (AI). Characterized by the resurgence of interest in neural network research and the development of powerful learning algorithms, deep learning has propelled AI to new heights, revolutionizing industries and transforming society in profound ways. In this comprehensive exploration, we delve into the origins, principles, advancements, applications, and implications of the deep learning revolution, shedding light on its profound impact on AI and beyond.

1. Origins and Principles of Deep Learning

Deep learning traces its roots back to the pioneering work of researchers in the 1940s and 1950s, who sought to model the structure and function of the human brain using computational models of interconnected neurons. However, early neural network research was limited by computational constraints and theoretical challenges, leading to a decline in interest in the 1960s and 1970s.

The resurgence of interest in neural networks came in the 1980s with the development of the backpropagation algorithm by Geoffrey Hinton, David Rumelhart, and Ronald Williams. Backpropagation enabled efficient training of multi-layer neural networks, known as "deep" neural networks, which could learn hierarchical representations of data.

The key principle behind deep learning is the hierarchical representation of data, where complex patterns and features are learned through multiple layers of abstraction. Each layer in a deep neural network learns to represent increasingly abstract features of the input data, enabling the network to capture complex relationships and make high-level predictions.

2. Advancements in Deep Learning

The deep learning revolution gained momentum in the early 2000s with the advent of large-scale datasets, powerful computational resources, and algorithmic innovations. Breakthroughs in areas such as image recognition, speech recognition, and natural language processing demonstrated the potential of deep learning to surpass human-level performance in various tasks.

One of the key advancements in deep learning was the development of convolutional neural networks (CNNs) for image recognition. CNNs leverage shared weights and local connectivity to efficiently learn spatial hierarchies of features from images, enabling state-of-the-art performance on tasks such as object detection and image classification.

In natural language processing, recurrent neural networks (RNNs) and attention mechanisms revolutionized the field by enabling the modeling of sequential data and long-range dependencies. RNNs are capable of processing sequences of variable length, making them well-suited for tasks such as machine translation, sentiment analysis, and speech recognition.

The advent of generative adversarial networks (GANs) introduced a new paradigm for training deep neural networks by pitting two networks against each other in a game-theoretic framework. GANs have been used to generate realistic images, videos, and audio samples, opening up new possibilities for creative applications and content generation.

3. Applications of Deep Learning

Deep learning has found applications in a wide range of domains and industries, including healthcare, finance, autonomous systems, and entertainment. In healthcare, deep learning algorithms have been deployed for tasks such as medical imaging analysis, disease diagnosis, and drug discovery, offering potential improvements in accuracy and efficiency over traditional methods.

In finance, deep learning models are used for tasks such as algorithmic trading, credit scoring, and fraud detection, leveraging large-scale financial data to make predictions and optimize decision-making processes. Autonomous systems, including self-driving cars, drones, and robotics, rely on deep learning algorithms for perception, navigation, and decision-making in complex and dynamic environments.

Deep learning has also revolutionized the entertainment industry, enabling advancements in areas such as computer graphics, virtual reality, and content generation. Generative models such as GANs have been used to create realistic visual effects, simulate virtual environments, and generate immersive experiences for users.

4. Implications and Challenges

The deep learning revolution has profound implications for society, technology, and the future of work. While deep learning has unlocked new capabilities and opportunities in various domains, it has also raised concerns about privacy, security, and ethical considerations surrounding the use of AI technologies.

One of the key challenges facing deep learning is the need for large-scale labeled datasets, which can be expensive and time-consuming to collect and annotate. Additionally, deep learning models are often characterized by their "black box" nature, making it difficult to interpret and explain their decisions, particularly in critical domains such as healthcare and finance.

Moreover, the reliance on large amounts of data and computational resources can exacerbate issues of data bias, algorithmic fairness, and environmental sustainability. Addressing these challenges will require interdisciplinary collaboration, regulatory oversight, and societal dialogue to ensure that deep learning technologies are developed and deployed responsibly.

5. Future Directions

As deep learning continues to evolve, researchers are exploring new directions and challenges in the field, including lifelong learning, meta-learning, and neuro-symbolic approaches. Lifelong learning aims to develop AI systems that can continuously adapt and learn from new data and experiences over time, enabling them to maintain relevance and performance in dynamic environments.

Meta-learning, or learning to learn, seeks to develop AI systems that can rapidly adapt to new tasks and domains with minimal human intervention, leveraging insights and knowledge gained from previous learning experiences. Neuro-symbolic approaches aim to integrate the strengths of symbolic reasoning and deep learning to develop AI systems that can reason, plan, and understand the world in a more human-like manner.

The deep learning revolution represents a transformative moment in the history of artificial intelligence, unleashing unprecedented capabilities and opportunities across industries and domains. While the deep learning paradigm has revolutionized AI research and applications, it also poses significant challenges and implications for society, technology, and the future of work. As researchers continue to push the boundaries of what is possible with deep learning, it is essential to remain vigilant and proactive in addressing ethical, societal, and

Reinforcement Learning: Teaching AI to Learn by Doing

Reinforcement learning (RL) stands as one of the most fascinating and promising branches of artificial intelligence (AI), emulating how humans and animals learn to make decisions through trial and error. Unlike supervised learning, where the model is trained on labeled data, and unsupervised learning, where the model discovers patterns in unlabeled data, reinforcement learning involves learning through interaction with an environment, receiving feedback in the form of rewards or punishments. In this extensive exploration, we delve into the origins, principles, algorithms, applications, challenges, and future directions of reinforcement learning, illuminating its transformative potential in reshaping AI systems.

1. Origins and Principles of Reinforcement Learning

The roots of reinforcement learning can be traced back to the fields of psychology and behavioral neuroscience, where researchers sought to understand how animals learn to navigate and survive in their environments. Inspired by behavioral experiments with animals, researchers in the 1950s and 1960s began to develop computational models of reinforcement learning, formalizing the principles of learning from feedback.

At the core of reinforcement learning is the concept of an agent interacting with an environment. The agent takes actions in the environment and receives feedback in the form of rewards or penalties, which it uses to learn and improve its decision-making policies. The goal of the agent is to maximize cumulative rewards over time by discovering optimal strategies for achieving its objectives.

Reinforcement learning is characterized by the exploration-exploitation trade-off, where the agent must balance the exploration of new actions to discover potentially better strategies with the exploitation of known actions that have yielded rewards in the past. This trade-off is essential for learning robust and adaptive policies that generalize well across different environments and tasks.

2. Algorithms and Techniques in Reinforcement Learning

Reinforcement learning encompasses a wide range of algorithms and techniques, ranging from simple value iteration and policy iteration methods to more sophisticated model-free approaches such as Q-learning, SARSA, and deep Q-networks (DQN). These algorithms differ in their assumptions, learning objectives, and computational requirements, but they all share the common goal of learning optimal decision-making policies through interaction with the environment.

One of the foundational algorithms in reinforcement learning is Q-learning, which learns a state-action value function, known as the Q-function, to estimate the expected cumulative reward of taking a particular action in a given state. Q-learning updates the Q-function iteratively based on observed rewards and transitions, converging to the optimal Q-values over time.

Deep Q-networks (DQN) extend Q-learning to high-dimensional state spaces by leveraging deep neural networks to approximate the Q-function. DQN has achieved remarkable success in solving complex reinforcement learning tasks, including playing Atari games at superhuman levels and mastering complex board games such as Go and chess.

Policy gradient methods offer an alternative approach to reinforcement learning, where the agent learns a parameterized policy that directly maps states to actions. By optimizing the policy parameters through gradient descent, policy gradient methods can learn stochastic policies that maximize expected cumulative rewards over time.

3. Applications of Reinforcement Learning

Reinforcement learning has found applications in a wide range of domains and industries, including robotics, autonomous systems, gaming, finance, healthcare, and recommendation systems. In robotics, reinforcement learning algorithms enable robots to learn complex manipulation tasks, locomotion, and navigation in dynamic and uncertain environments.

Autonomous systems, such as self-driving cars, drones, and robotic agents, rely on reinforcement learning algorithms for perception, planning, and decision-making. Reinforcement learning enables these systems to learn from experience and adapt to changing conditions, leading to safer and more efficient autonomous operation.

In gaming, reinforcement learning has achieved significant breakthroughs in training AI agents to play complex strategy games such as chess, Go, and Dota 2. AlphaGo, developed by DeepMind, made headlines by defeating world champion Go players, demonstrating the power of reinforcement learning in mastering strategic decision-making tasks.

In finance, reinforcement learning algorithms are used for portfolio optimization, algorithmic trading, and risk management. These algorithms analyze historical market data, learn patterns and trends, and make decisions to maximize returns or minimize risk, leading to improved investment strategies and decision-making processes.

In healthcare, reinforcement learning has applications in personalized medicine, drug discovery, and treatment optimization. Reinforcement learning algorithms can learn from patient data to recommend personalized treatment plans, optimize drug dosages, and identify effective interventions for chronic diseases.

4. Challenges and Limitations

Despite its remarkable successes, reinforcement learning faces several challenges and limitations that hinder its widespread adoption and applicability in real-world settings. One of the primary challenges is sample efficiency—the amount of data and experience required for the agent to learn effective policies. Reinforcement learning algorithms often require large amounts of training data and computational resources to achieve good performance, which can be impractical or costly in certain domains

Another challenge is the issue of exploration versus exploitation, where the agent must balance the exploration of new actions with the exploitation of known actions to maximize cumulative rewards. Designing effective exploration strategies that balance the need for exploration with the desire for exploitation remains an ongoing research challenge in reinforcement learning.

The curse of dimensionality poses a significant challenge in reinforcement learning, particularly in high-dimensional state and action spaces. As the dimensionality of the state

Chapter 3
Understanding Neural Networks

In the ever-expanding realm of artificial intelligence, neural networks stand as one of the most fascinating and influential technologies. Born from the aspiration to mimic the human brain's extraordinary computational power, neural networks have revolutionized various fields, from computer vision to natural language processing. "Understanding Neural Networks" embarks on a journey to unravel the intricacies of these complex systems, shedding light on their architecture, functioning, training methods, and applications.

Neural networks, inspired by the biological neurons of the human brain, consist of interconnected layers of artificial neurons, each contributing to the network's ability to learn from data and make predictions. As we delve into the depths of neural networks, we will explore their fundamental principles, including feedforward and recurrent architectures, activation functions, and learning algorithms.

This chapter serves as a gateway to the world of neural networks, offering readers a comprehensive understanding of their inner workings and potential. From simple perceptrons to deep convolutional networks and recurrent models, the journey through neural networks promises to unveil their power, versatility, and transformative impact on AI and beyond. Join us as we embark on a voyage of discovery into the heart of neural networks, where intelligence meets innovation.

Introduction to Neurons and Synapses

Neurons and synapses are the building blocks of the nervous system, forming the intricate network that underpins all brain functions, from basic reflexes to complex cognitive processes. Understanding the structure and function of neurons and synapses is essential for unraveling the mysteries of the brain and developing artificial intelligence systems inspired by its principles. In this detailed exploration, we delve into the anatomy, physiology, and computational properties of neurons and synapses, shedding light on their fundamental roles in information processing and cognition.

1. Anatomy of Neurons

Neurons, also known as nerve cells, are the basic functional units of the nervous system. They are specialized cells that transmit electrical and chemical signals throughout the body, enabling communication between different parts of the nervous system and orchestrating a wide range of physiological and behavioral responses.

1.1. Neuronal Structure

Neurons consist of three main parts: the cell body (soma), dendrites, and axon. The cell body contains the nucleus and organelles responsible for maintaining the cell's metabolic functions. Dendrites are branched extensions that receive incoming signals from other neurons and transmit them to the cell body. The axon is a long, slender projection that carries electrical impulses away from the cell body to other neurons or target cells.

1.2. Types of Neurons

There are several types of neurons, each with distinct anatomical and functional characteristics. Sensory neurons transmit sensory information from the peripheral nervous system to the central nervous system. Motor neurons transmit signals from the central nervous system to muscles and glands, controlling voluntary and involuntary movements. Interneurons, or associative neurons, facilitate communication between sensory and motor neurons, integrating and processing information within the central nervous system.

2. Physiology of Neurons

Neurons communicate with each other and with other cells through electrical and chemical signals. The process of neural communication, known as synaptic transmission, occurs at specialized junctions called synapses, where neurotransmitters are released from the presynaptic neuron and bind to receptors on the postsynaptic neuron, triggering electrical changes in the postsynaptic neuron.

2.1. Action Potential

The fundamental unit of electrical signaling in neurons is the action potential, a rapid and transient change in membrane potential that propagates along the axon. Action potentials are generated when the membrane potential of the neuron reaches a threshold level, causing voltage-gated ion channels to open and allowing sodium ions to flow into the cell, depolarizing the membrane. This depolarization triggers the opening of additional voltage-gated ion channels, leading to the propagation of the action potential along the axon.

2.2. Synaptic Transmission

Synaptic transmission occurs when an action potential reaches the presynaptic terminal of a neuron, causing the release of neurotransmitters into the synaptic cleft. Neurotransmitters diffuse across the synaptic cleft and bind to receptors on the postsynaptic neuron, altering its membrane potential and modulating its excitability. Excitatory neurotransmitters depolarize the postsynaptic neuron, making it more likely to generate an action potential, while inhibitory neurotransmitters hyperpolarize the postsynaptic neuron, making it less likely to generate an action potential.

3. Computational Properties of Neurons and Synapses

Neurons and synapses exhibit complex computational properties that enable them to process and integrate information in sophisticated ways. These computational properties are crucial for various brain functions, including sensory processing, motor control, learning, and memory.

Neurons integrate synaptic inputs from thousands of presynaptic neurons, summing the excitatory and inhibitory signals they receive to determine whether to generate an action potential. This process of synaptic integration is influenced by factors such as the location and timing of synaptic inputs, the strength of synaptic connections, and the membrane properties of the neuron.

3.1. Plasticity and Learning

Synaptic plasticity, the ability of synapses to strengthen or weaken in response to activity, is a fundamental mechanism underlying learning and memory in the brain. Long-term potentiation (LTP) and long-term depression (LTD) are two forms of synaptic plasticity that involve the strengthening or weakening of synaptic connections, respectively, through changes in synaptic efficacy.

3.2. Neural Circuits and Networks

Neurons are organized into complex networks of interconnected circuits that process information in parallel and hierarchical fashion. These neural circuits exhibit emergent properties that arise from the interactions between individual neurons, enabling the brain to perform complex computations, such as pattern recognition, decision-making, and language processing.

4. Applications and Implications

The study of neurons and synapses has far-reaching applications and implications in various fields, including neuroscience, medicine, and artificial intelligence.

4.1. Neuroscience

Understanding the structure and function of neurons and synapses is essential for advancing our knowledge of the brain and its role in behavior, cognition, and disease. Neuroscientists use techniques such as electrophysiology, neuroimaging, and optogenetics to study neural activity and connectivity in both healthy and diseased brains, with the aim of developing new therapies for neurological and psychiatric disorders.

4.2. Medicine

Neurological and psychiatric disorders, such as Alzheimer's disease, Parkinson's disease, epilepsy, and depression, are characterized by abnormalities in neuronal structure and function. By elucidating the underlying mechanisms of these disorders, researchers hope to develop novel diagnostic tools and therapeutic interventions that target specific neuronal pathways and synaptic connections.

4.3. Artificial Intelligence

Neural networks, inspired by the structure and function of biological neurons and synapses, have emerged as powerful tools for solving complex computational problems in artificial intelligence. Deep learning, a subfield of machine learning based on artificial neural networks, has achieved remarkable success in tasks such as image recognition, natural language processing, and autonomous driving, by emulating the principles of synaptic plasticity and neural computation.

Neurons and synapses are the fundamental building blocks of the nervous system, responsible for encoding, transmitting, and processing information in the brain. By understanding the anatomy, physiology, and computational properties of neurons and synapses, researchers can unravel the mysteries of the brain and develop new insights into cognition, behavior, and disease. Moreover, the study of neurons and synapses has far-reaching applications in fields such as neuroscience, medicine, and artificial intelligence, shaping our understanding of the mind and inspiring new technologies that emulate the brain's remarkable capabilities.

Feedforward Neural Networks: Unraveling the Basics

Feedforward neural networks (FNNs) represent one of the fundamental architectures in artificial neural networks, serving as the cornerstone for various applications in machine learning, pattern recognition, and data analysis. Rooted in the principles of biological neurons and inspired by the human brain's information processing capabilities, FNNs have emerged as powerful tools for solving complex problems in diverse domains. In this comprehensive exploration, we delve into the anatomy, functioning, training methods, and applications of feedforward neural networks, shedding light on their underlying mechanisms and practical utility.

1. Anatomy of Feedforward Neural Networks

At the core of feedforward neural networks lie layers of interconnected artificial neurons, organized into an input layer, one or more hidden layers, and an output layer. Each neuron in the network is connected to neurons in adjacent layers through weighted connections, which transmit signals from one layer to the next. The architecture of FNNs is characterized by its feedforward nature, where information flows only in one direction—from the input layer through the hidden layers to the output layer—without any feedback loops or recurrent connections.

1.1. Input Layer

The input layer of an FNN serves as the entry point for external data or features that are fed into the network for processing. Each neuron in the input layer represents a feature or attribute of the input data, and its activation value corresponds to the magnitude of the input signal. The input layer acts as a conduit for passing information from the external environment to the hidden layers of the network.

1.2. Hidden Layers

The hidden layers of an FNN are responsible for extracting and transforming the input data into higher-level representations that capture complex patterns and relationships. Each neuron in a hidden layer receives inputs from neurons in the previous layer, applies a nonlinear transformation to the inputs using an activation function, and passes the transformed outputs to neurons in the next layer. The number and size of hidden layers in an FNN can vary depending on the complexity of the problem and the desired level of abstraction.

1.3. Output Layer

The output layer of an FNN generates the final predictions or outputs based on the transformed representations learned by the hidden layers. Each neuron in the output layer corresponds to a class label, regression target, or decision outcome, and its activation value represents the network's confidence or certainty in predicting the corresponding output. The output layer serves as the interface between the internal representations learned by the network and the external task or objective being solved.

2. Functioning of Feedforward Neural Networks

The functioning of feedforward neural networks involves two main processes: forward propagation and backward propagation.

2.1. Forward Propagation

Forward propagation is the process by which input signals are propagated forward through the network, layer by layer, to generate predictions or outputs. It begins with the input layer, where external data is fed into the network, and proceeds through each hidden layer, where the input signals are transformed and passed to the next layer, until reaching the output layer, where the final predictions are generated based on the network's learned representations.

2.2. Backward Propagation

Backward propagation, also known as backpropagation, is the process by which errors or discrepancies between the predicted outputs and the true targets are propagated backward through the network to update the network's parameters and minimize the prediction errors. It involves computing the gradients of the loss function with respect to the network's parameters, such as the weights and biases, and using these gradients to adjust the parameters in the direction that reduces the prediction errors.

3. Training Methods for Feedforward Neural Networks

Training feedforward neural networks involves iteratively adjusting the network's parameters to minimize a predefined loss function, which measures the discrepancy between the predicted outputs and the true targets. Several training methods and optimization algorithms are commonly used to train FNNs effectively.

3.1. Gradient Descent

Gradient descent is a widely used optimization algorithm for training FNNs, which iteratively updates the network's parameters in the direction of the steepest descent of the loss function. It computes the gradients of the loss function with respect to the network's parameters using backpropagation and updates the parameters by taking small steps in the opposite direction of the gradients.

3.2. Stochastic Gradient Descent (SGD)

Stochastic gradient descent is a variant of gradient descent that updates the network's parameters using mini-batches of training samples rather than the entire dataset. It randomly samples a subset of training samples at each iteration, computes the gradients of the loss function with respect to the parameters using the sampled mini-batch, and updates the parameters accordingly. SGD is computationally efficient and well-suited for large-scale datasets.

3.3. Adam Optimizer

Adam (Adaptive Moment Estimation) is an adaptive optimization algorithm that combines the advantages of gradient descent and momentum-based optimization. It maintains per-parameter learning rates and adapts the learning rates dynamically based on the gradients and past update history of the parameters. Adam is known for its robustness and efficiency in training deep neural networks.

4. Applications of Feedforward Neural Networks

Feedforward neural networks have found applications in various domains and fields, ranging from image and speech recognition to natural language processing, healthcare, finance, and beyond.

4.1. Image and Speech Recognition

Feedforward neural networks, particularly convolutional neural networks (CNNs), are widely used for image and speech recognition tasks. CNNs excel at capturing spatial hierarchies of features in images and temporal patterns in audio signals, making them well-suited for tasks such as object detection, image classification, speech recognition, and speaker identification.

4.2. Natural Language Processing (NLP)

In natural language processing, feedforward neural networks, recurrent neural networks (RNNs), and transformer models are used for various tasks, including language modeling, sentiment analysis, machine translation, and text generation. These models leverage the hierarchical structure of language and the sequential nature of text data to extract meaningful representations and generate accurate predictions.

4.3. Healthcare and Finance

In healthcare, feedforward neural networks are used for tasks such as disease diagnosis, medical image analysis, drug discovery, and personalized treatment recommendation. In finance, they are employed for tasks such as fraud detection, credit scoring, risk assessment, and algorithmic trading, leveraging large-scale financial data to make informed decisions and predictions.

Feedforward neural networks represent a powerful class of artificial neural networks that have revolutionized various fields and domains. With their ability to learn complex patterns and relationships from data, FNNs have become indispensable tools for solving a wide range of problems in machine learning, pattern recognition, and data analysis. As research in neural networks continues to advance, feedforward neural networks are expected to play an increasingly important role in shaping the future of artificial intelligence and driving innovation in diverse areas of science and technology.

Convolutional Neural Networks (CNNs): Unraveling the Power of Visual Perception

Convolutional Neural Networks (CNNs) stand at the forefront of modern artificial intelligence, particularly in the domain of computer vision. These specialized neural networks have demonstrated remarkable capabilities in tasks such as image classification, object detection, facial recognition, and medical image analysis. Inspired by the structure and function of the visual cortex in the human brain, CNNs are designed to efficiently process and analyze visual data, making them indispensable tools in a wide range of applications. In this comprehensive exploration, we delve into the anatomy, functioning, architectures, training methods, and applications of Convolutional Neural Networks, shedding light on their transformative potential in reshaping the landscape of computer vision and beyond.

1. Anatomy of Convolutional Neural Networks

At the heart of Convolutional Neural Networks lie layers of specialized neurons, organized into distinct modules designed to extract and process visual features from input images.

1.1. Convolutional Layers

The cornerstone of CNNs, convolutional layers, perform feature extraction by convolving input images with a set of learnable filters, also known as kernels or feature detectors. Each filter applies a convolution operation to a small region of the input image, extracting local patterns and features such as edges, textures, and shapes. By stacking multiple convolutional layers, CNNs can learn hierarchical representations of visual features, capturing increasingly complex and abstract information as they progress deeper into the network.

1.2. Pooling Layers

Pooling layers, often interleaved with convolutional layers, reduce the spatial dimensions of feature maps while preserving the most salient features. Common pooling operations include max pooling, where the maximum value within each pooling region is retained, and average pooling, where the average value is computed instead. Pooling layers help improve the computational efficiency of CNNs, reduce the number of parameters, and enhance the network's robustness to translation and distortion invariance.

1.3. Fully Connected Layers

At the end of the convolutional backbone, fully connected layers serve as the decision-making component of the CNN. These layers consist of densely connected neurons, where each neuron is connected to every neuron in the preceding layer. Fully connected layers integrate the high-level features learned by the convolutional layers and generate the final output predictions or classifications. They are typically followed by activation functions such as softmax for multi-class classification or sigmoid for binary classification.

2. Functioning of Convolutional Neural Networks

The functioning of Convolutional Neural Networks involves two main processes: forward propagation and backpropagation.

2.1. Forward Propagation

Forward propagation is the process by which input images are fed into the network and pass through successive layers of convolution, pooling, and fully connected operations to generate predictions or classifications. It begins with the convolutional layers, where the input images are convolved with learnable filters to extract local features. The resulting feature maps are then downsampled and aggregated through pooling layers to reduce spatial dimensions and extract the most salient features. Finally, the high-level representations learned by the convolutional layers are flattened and fed into fully connected layers to generate the final output predictions.

2.2. Backpropagation

Backpropagation, or backward propagation of errors, is the process by which prediction errors are propagated backward through the network to update the network's parameters and minimize prediction discrepancies. It involves computing the gradients of the loss function with respect to the network's parameters using the chain rule of calculus and adjusting the parameters in the opposite direction of the gradients using optimization algorithms such as stochastic gradient descent (SGD) or Adam.

3. Architectures of Convolutional Neural Networks

Convolutional Neural Networks come in various architectures and configurations, each tailored to specific tasks and objectives. Some of the most popular architectures include:

3.1. LeNet-5

One of the pioneering CNN architectures, LeNet-5, was developed by Yann LeCun et al. for handwritten digit recognition tasks. It consists of several convolutional and pooling layers followed by fully connected layers, demonstrating the efficacy of CNNs in pattern recognition tasks.

3.2. AlexNet

AlexNet, introduced by Alex Krizhevsky et al., marked a breakthrough in image classification by winning the ImageNet Large Scale Visual Recognition Challenge in 2012. It consists of multiple convolutional layers with rectified linear unit (ReLU) activation functions, local response normalization, and max-pooling layers, followed by fully connected layers.

3.3. VGGNet

VGGNet, proposed by Karen Simonyan and Andrew Zisserman, is characterized by its simplicity and uniform architecture, comprising multiple stacked convolutional layers with small 3x3 filters and max-pooling layers. VGGNet achieved excellent performance on image classification tasks while maintaining a straightforward and interpretable architecture.

3.4. ResNet

Residual Networks (ResNets), introduced by Kaiming He et al., introduced the concept of residual learning, where shortcut connections, or skip connections, are added to the network to facilitate the flow of gradients and alleviate the vanishing gradient problem. ResNets achieved state-of-the-art performance on image classification tasks with significantly deeper architectures.

4. Training Methods for Convolutional Neural Networks

Training Convolutional Neural Networks involves optimizing the network's parameters to minimize a predefined loss function using optimization algorithms such as stochastic gradient descent (SGD) or adaptive optimization algorithms like Adam. Several techniques and strategies are employed to improve the training efficiency and effectiveness of CNNs:

4.1. Data Augmentation

Data augmentation techniques such as random cropping, rotation, flipping, and scaling are used to artificially increase the diversity and variability of the training data, thereby reducing overfitting and improving the generalization performance of CNNs.

4.2. Transfer Learning

Transfer learning involves leveraging pre-trained CNN models on large-scale datasets such as ImageNet and fine-tuning them on target tasks with limited labeled data. By transferring knowledge learned from one task to another, transfer learning enables CNNs to achieve better performance and faster convergence on new

Recurrent Neural Networks (RNNs): Modeling Temporal Dynamics

Recurrent Neural Networks (RNNs) represent a class of neural networks specifically designed to model sequential data and capture temporal dependencies. Unlike feedforward neural networks, which process fixed-size inputs independently of their order, RNNs maintain an internal state that allows them to incorporate information from previous time steps into their computations. This property makes RNNs well-suited for a wide range of tasks involving sequential data, such as natural language processing, time series prediction, speech recognition, and more. In this comprehensive exploration, we delve into the anatomy, functioning, architectures, training methods, and applications of Recurrent Neural Networks, shedding light on their unique ability to model temporal dynamics and capture complex patterns in sequential data.

1. Anatomy of Recurrent Neural Networks

At the core of Recurrent Neural Networks lie recurrent connections, which enable them to maintain a memory of previous inputs and incorporate this information into their current computations.

1.1. Recurrent Connections

Recurrent connections are a defining feature of RNNs, allowing information to persist over time and be passed from one time step to the next. These connections create loops within the network architecture, allowing neurons to receive inputs not only from the current time step but also from previous time steps. This recurrent structure enables RNNs to capture temporal dependencies and process sequential data in a dynamic and context-sensitive manner.

1.2. Hidden State

The hidden state, or internal state, of an RNN represents the network's memory of past inputs and computations. At each time step, the hidden state is updated based on the current input and the previous hidden state, allowing the network to retain information about the sequence of inputs it has observed so far. The hidden state serves as a compact representation of the input history and influences the network's predictions and decisions at each time step.

1.3. Time Unfolding

To facilitate training and computation, RNNs are often "unfolded" over time into a series of interconnected layers, each corresponding to a specific time step in the sequence. This unfolding creates a deep, layered structure that allows gradients to flow through the network more efficiently during training. Each layer in the unfolded RNN corresponds to a recurrence of the same set of parameters, enabling the network to process sequences of arbitrary length.

2. Functioning of Recurrent Neural Networks

The functioning of Recurrent Neural Networks involves two main processes: forward propagation and backpropagation through time (BPTT).

2.1. Forward Propagation

Forward propagation in RNNs is similar to that in feedforward neural networks, with the addition of recurrent connections that allow information to flow from one time step to the next. At each time step, the current input is combined with the previous hidden state to compute the new hidden state and generate the output prediction. This process is repeated for each time step in the sequence, allowing the network to process the entire input sequence and generate a sequence of output predictions.

2.2. Backpropagation Through Time (BPTT)

Backpropagation through time (BPTT) is an extension of the backpropagation algorithm used to train RNNs. It involves unfolding the network over time, computing the gradients of the loss function with respect to the network's parameters at each time step, and then backpropagating these gradients through the unfolded network to update the parameters. BPTT effectively extends backpropagation to sequences of arbitrary length, allowing RNNs to learn from input sequences of varying lengths and capture long-term dependencies.

3. Architectures of Recurrent Neural Networks

Several architectures of Recurrent Neural Networks have been developed, each with its own strengths and limitations. Some of the most common architectures include:

3.1. Vanilla RNNs

Vanilla RNNs are the simplest form of recurrent neural networks, consisting of a single recurrent layer with a tanh activation function. Despite their simplicity, vanilla RNNs suffer from the vanishing gradient problem, where gradients diminish exponentially over long sequences, making it difficult for the network to capture long-term dependencies.

3.2. Long Short-Term Memory (LSTM) Networks

Long Short-Term Memory (LSTM) networks address the vanishing gradient problem by introducing specialized memory cells and gating mechanisms that allow the network to retain information over long periods of time. LSTM networks consist of multiple memory cells, each equipped with input, output, and forget gates that control the flow of information into, out of, and within the cell. This gating mechanism enables LSTM networks to learn and store long-term dependencies more effectively than vanilla RNNs.

3.3. Gated Recurrent Unit (GRU) Networks

Gated Recurrent Unit (GRU) networks are a simplified version of LSTM networks that combine the input and forget gates into a single update gate, reducing the computational complexity of the model. GRU networks retain much of the effectiveness of LSTM networks while being more computationally efficient and easier to train.

4. Training Methods for Recurrent Neural Networks

Training Recurrent Neural Networks involves optimizing the network's parameters to minimize a predefined loss function using optimization algorithms such as stochastic gradient descent (SGD) or adaptive optimization algorithms like Adam. Several techniques and strategies are employed to improve the training efficiency and effectiveness of RNNs:

4.1. Gradient Clipping

Gradient clipping is a regularization technique used to prevent exploding gradients during training by capping the magnitude of the gradients to a predefined threshold. This helps stabilize the training process and prevent numerical instabilities caused by excessively large gradients.

4.2. Truncated Backpropagation Through Time (TBPTT)

Truncated Backpropagation Through Time (TB

Chapter 4
Machine Learning: From Theory to Practice

Machine learning stands as a cornerstone of modern technology, offering powerful tools to extract insights, make predictions, and automate decision-making processes across various domains. From its theoretical underpinnings to its practical applications, the journey through machine learning encompasses a diverse array of algorithms, methodologies, and techniques. "Machine Learning: From Theory to Practice" embarks on a comprehensive exploration of this dynamic field, bridging the gap between theoretical concepts and real-world applications

In this chapter, we delve into the fundamental principles of machine learning, elucidating key concepts such as supervised learning, unsupervised learning, reinforcement learning, and deep learning. We explore the theoretical foundations of these concepts, including optimization theory, probabilistic modeling, and statistical inference, providing readers with a solid understanding of the underlying principles that govern machine learning algorithms.

Furthermore, we transition from theory to practice by examining practical considerations in machine learning, such as data preprocessing, feature engineering, model selection, and evaluation metrics. Through case studies, examples, and hands-on exercises, we illustrate how machine learning techniques are applied to solve real-world problems in domains such as healthcare, finance, marketing, and more.

Join us on a journey through the intricate landscape of machine learning, where theory meets practice, and innovation knows no bounds. Whether you're a novice exploring the fundamentals or an expert seeking practical insights, this chapter promises to deepen your understanding of machine learning and its transformative impact on the world around us.

Supervised Learning: Training with Labeled Data

Supervised learning stands as one of the foundational pillars of machine learning, offering a powerful framework for training predictive models from labeled data. In supervised learning, the algorithm learns to map input data to output labels based on examples provided during the training phase. This paradigm enables the model to generalize its predictions to unseen data, making it applicable to a wide range of tasks, from classification to regression and beyond. In this detailed exploration, we delve into the principles, algorithms, methodologies, and practical considerations of supervised learning, shedding light on its inner workings and real-world applications.

1. Introduction to Supervised Learning

Supervised learning revolves around the notion of learning from labeled data, where each training example consists of a pair comprising an input feature vector and its corresponding output label or target variable. The goal is to learn a mapping function from the input space to the output space that accurately predicts the labels of unseen data points.

1.1. The Supervised Learning Problem

Formally, the supervised learning problem can be defined as follows: given a training dataset $D = \{(x^{(i)}, y^{(i)})\}_{i=1}^{N}$, where $x^{(i)}$ denotes the ith input feature vector and $y^{(i)}$ denotes its corresponding output label, the task is to learn a function $f: \mathcal{X} \rightarrow \mathcal{Y}$ that maps input instances to output labels, such that $f(x^{(i)}) \approx y^{(i)}$ for all i in the dataset.

2. Types of Supervised Learning

Supervised learning can be broadly categorized into two main types: classification and regression.

2.1. Classification

In classification tasks, the output variable y belongs to a discrete set of classes or categories. The goal is to learn a mapping from input features to class labels, enabling the model to classify unseen instances into predefined categories. Common examples of classification tasks include email spam detection, sentiment analysis, image recognition, and medical diagnosis.

2.2. Regression

In regression tasks, the output variable y is continuous or numerical. The goal is to learn a mapping from input features to numerical values, enabling the model to predict a quantitative outcome. Regression models are widely used in domains such as finance, economics, engineering, and healthcare for tasks such as stock price prediction, housing price estimation, demand forecasting, and patient outcome prediction.

3. Algorithms and Models in Supervised Learning

Supervised learning encompasses a diverse array of algorithms and models, each with its own strengths, limitations, and applications.

3.1. Linear Models

Linear models are simple yet powerful algorithms that assume a linear relationship between the input features and the output variable. Examples include linear regression for regression tasks and logistic regression for binary classification tasks. Despite their simplicity, linear models are widely used in practice due to their interpretability, efficiency, and scalability.

3.2. Decision Trees

Decision trees are hierarchical tree-like structures that recursively partition the feature space into regions, based on the values of input features, to make predictions. Each internal node represents a decision based on a feature, and each leaf node represents a class label or numerical value. Decision trees are intuitive, easy to interpret, and capable of capturing nonlinear relationships in the data.

3.3. Ensemble Methods

Ensemble methods combine multiple base models to improve predictive performance and robustness. Examples include Random Forests, which aggregate the predictions of multiple decision trees, and Gradient Boosting Machines (GBM), which sequentially fit weak learners to the residuals of the preceding models. Ensemble methods are highly effective in practice and often yield state-of-the-art results in various machine learning competitions and benchmarks.

3.4. Neural Networks

Neural networks represent a class of powerful nonlinear models inspired by the structure and function of the human brain. Deep neural networks, in particular, have achieved remarkable success in supervised learning tasks, thanks to their ability to automatically learn hierarchical representations of data. Convolutional Neural Networks (CNNs) excel in image classification and object recognition tasks, while Recurrent Neural Networks (RNNs) are well-suited for sequential data such as natural language processing and time series prediction.

4. Training and Evaluation in Supervised Learning

Training a supervised learning model involves optimizing its parameters to minimize a predefined loss function, typically using gradient-based optimization algorithms such as stochastic gradient descent (SGD) or variants like Adam and RMSprop. The model is trained on a labeled training dataset, and its performance is evaluated on a separate validation or test dataset using appropriate evaluation metrics.

4.1. Data Splitting

To assess the generalization performance of a supervised learning model, the available data is typically split into three disjoint sets: a training set for model training, a validation set for hyperparameter tuning and model selection, and a test set for final evaluation. This ensures that the model's performance is accurately assessed on unseen data.

4.2. Evaluation Metrics

Various evaluation metrics are used to assess the performance of supervised learning models, depending on the task and the nature of the output variable. For classification tasks, common metrics include accuracy, precision, recall, F1 score, and area under the receiver operating characteristic curve (AUC-ROC). For regression tasks, common metrics include mean squared error (MSE), mean absolute error (MAE), R-squared (R^2), and root mean squared error (RMSE).

5. Applications of Supervised Learning

Supervised learning finds applications in a wide range of domains and industries, including but not limited to:

- **Healthcare:** Predicting disease risk, diagnosing medical conditions, and personalizing treatment plans.

- **Finance:** Credit scoring, fraud detection, stock price prediction, and algorithmic trading.
- **Marketing:** Customer segmentation, churn prediction, recommendation systems, and targeted advertising.
- **Natural Language Processing (NLP):** Text classification, sentiment analysis, machine translation, and named entity recognition.
- **Computer Vision:** Object detection, image segmentation, facial recognition, and autonomous driving.

6. Challenges and Future Directions

Despite its successes, supervised learning still faces several challenges, such as overfitting, data scarcity, class imbalance, and interpretability. Addressing these challenges requires advances in algorithm design, data collection, and model evaluation. Additionally, emerging trends such as semi-supervised learning, active learning, and continual learning offer promising avenues for future research and innovation in supervised learning.

supervised learning stands as a cornerstone of modern machine learning, providing a powerful framework for training predictive models from labeled data. From classification and regression algorithms to neural networks and ensemble methods, the arsenal of supervised learning techniques continues to grow, enabling us to tackle increasingly complex and diverse real-world problems with ever-improving accuracy and efficiency.

Unsupervised Learning: Discovering Hidden Patterns

Unsupervised learning represents a pivotal paradigm within the realm of machine learning, focusing on the exploration and extraction of underlying structures and patterns from unlabeled data. Unlike supervised learning, which relies on labeled examples to infer relationships between inputs and outputs, unsupervised learning operates on raw, unlabeled data, seeking to uncover latent representations and organize information in a meaningful manner. In this comprehensive exploration, we delve into the principles, algorithms, methodologies, and practical applications of unsupervised learning, elucidating its significance in uncovering hidden insights and driving innovation across diverse domains.

1. Introduction to Unsupervised Learning

Unsupervised learning constitutes a fundamental branch of machine learning, distinguished by its ability to discern intrinsic structures and patterns within data without explicit supervision. In contrast to supervised learning, where models are trained on labeled examples to predict outcomes, unsupervised learning aims to unveil underlying relationships, clusters, or representations inherent in the data itself. This paradigm empowers practitioners to extract valuable insights, detect anomalies, and uncover novel knowledge from raw, unlabeled datasets, making it indispensable in exploratory data analysis and knowledge discovery.

1.1. The Unsupervised Learning Problem

The core objective of unsupervised learning is to infer the underlying structure or organization of data in the absence of explicit labels or target variables. Formally, given an unlabeled dataset $X = \{x^{(1)}, x^{(2)}, \ldots, x^{(N)}\}$, the goal is to learn a mapping or representation that captures the inherent patterns, dependencies, or clusters within the data points. Unsupervised learning tasks encompass a wide spectrum of endeavors, including clustering, dimensionality reduction, density estimation, and generative modeling.

2. Types of Unsupervised Learning

Unsupervised learning encompasses diverse methodologies tailored to distinct objectives and data characteristics. Some of the prominent types of unsupervised learning include clustering, dimensionality reduction, and generative modeling.

2.1. Clustering

Clustering entails partitioning data points into coherent groups or clusters based on similarity or proximity metrics. The primary aim is to identify natural groupings within the data, enabling practitioners to uncover intrinsic structures or segments. Common clustering algorithms include K-means clustering, hierarchical clustering, DBSCAN (Density-Based Spatial Clustering of Applications with Noise), and Gaussian mixture models (GMMs).

2.2. Dimensionality Reduction

Dimensionality reduction techniques aim to reduce the complexity and dimensionality of high-dimensional data while preserving essential information and structures. By projecting data onto lower-dimensional spaces or subspaces, dimensionality reduction facilitates visualization, compression, and computational efficiency. Principal Component Analysis (PCA), t-Distributed Stochastic Neighbor Embedding (t-SNE), and autoencoders are popular methods for dimensionality reduction.

2.3. Generative Modeling

Generative modeling focuses on learning the underlying probability distribution of the data to generate new samples or instances that resemble the original data distribution. These models capture the intrinsic patterns and dependencies within the data, enabling the synthesis of novel and realistic data points. Notable generative models include Variational Autoencoders (VAEs), Generative Adversarial Networks (GANs), and autoregressive models such as PixelCNN and WaveNet.

3. Algorithms and Models in Unsupervised Learning

A myriad of algorithms and models have been developed to address the challenges and objectives of unsupervised learning tasks. These methodologies leverage diverse mathematical frameworks and computational techniques to extract meaningful representations and structures from unlabeled data.

3.1. K-means Clustering

K-means clustering is a popular algorithm for partitioning data into k distinct clusters based on centroids or cluster centers. It iteratively assigns data points to the nearest centroid and updates the centroids based on the mean of the assigned points. K-means clustering is efficient, scalable, and widely used in various applications, including customer segmentation, image compression, and anomaly detection.

3.2. Principal Component Analysis (PCA)

Principal Component Analysis (PCA) is a dimensionality reduction technique that projects high-dimensional data onto a lower-dimensional subspace while preserving maximal variance. PCA identifies the principal axes or components of variation within the data and projects data points onto these components. It is widely employed for feature extraction, data visualization, and noise reduction in diverse domains.

3.3. Variational Autoencoders (VAEs)

Variational Autoencoders (VAEs) are generative models that learn latent representations of data by mapping inputs to a lower-dimensional latent space and reconstructing them back to the original space. VAEs leverage variational inference to approximate the posterior distribution of latent variables, enabling the generation of new samples and the interpolation between data points. VAEs are versatile and capable of generating diverse and realistic samples across different domains.

4. Training and Evaluation in Unsupervised Learning

Training unsupervised learning models involves optimizing model parameters to capture the underlying structures or representations within the data. Unlike supervised learning, where labeled examples are used to compute loss functions, unsupervised learning often relies on intrinsic properties of the data, such as proximity or reconstruction error, for training and evaluation.

4.1. Objective Functions

Unsupervised learning models are typically trained using objective functions that quantify the agreement between observed data and model-generated outputs. Common objective functions include clustering criteria such as inertia in K-means clustering, reconstruction loss in autoencoders, and likelihood-based measures in generative modeling.

4.2. Evaluation Metrics

Evaluating the performance of unsupervised learning models can be challenging due to the absence of ground truth labels. Consequently, evaluation metrics often focus on intrinsic properties of the learned representations or structures, such as clustering quality, reconstruction error, or likelihood scores. External validation techniques, such as silhouette analysis for clustering or visualization methods for dimensionality reduction, can also provide insights into the effectiveness of unsupervised learning models.

5. Applications of Unsupervised Learning

Unsupervised learning finds applications across a myriad of domains and industries, offering valuable insights, discovering hidden patterns, and facilitating decision-making processes. Some prominent applications include:

- Market segmentation and customer profiling in marketing and retail.
- Anomaly detection and fraud detection in cybersecurity and finance.
- Image clustering and content-based image retrieval in computer vision.
- Topic modeling and document clustering in natural language processing.
- Drug discovery and molecular modeling in pharmaceuticals and healthcare.

6. Challenges and Future Directions

Despite its versatility and utility, unsupervised learning encounters several challenges, including scalability, interpretability, and robustness to noisy or high-dimensional data. Addressing these challenges requires advances in algorithmic design, computational methodologies, and theoretical foundations. Additionally, emerging trends such as self-supervised learning, semi-supervised learning, and unsupervised meta-learning offer promising avenues for future research and innovation in unsupervised learning.

In summary, unsupervised learning stands as a cornerstone of machine learning, enabling practitioners to unveil hidden structures, extract valuable insights, and derive actionable knowledge from unlabeled data. By leveraging clustering, dimensionality reduction, and generative modeling techniques, unsupervised learning empowers researchers, analysts, and practitioners to navigate the complexities of real-world data and unlock the potential of untapped information sources. As the field continues to evolve, unsupervised learning holds the promise of further revolutionizing how we perceive, analyze, and derive meaning from the vast troves of unstructured data that surround us.

Reinforcement Learning Algorithms: Navigating the Exploration-Exploitation Trade-off

Reinforcement learning (RL) stands as a paradigm within machine learning that focuses on learning optimal decision-making policies through interaction with an environment. Unlike supervised and unsupervised learning, which rely on labeled or unlabeled data, RL agents learn by receiving feedback in the form of rewards or penalties as they navigate and explore their environment. In this detailed exploration, we delve into the principles, algorithms, methodologies, and practical applications of reinforcement learning, shedding light on its dynamic nature and transformative potential in diverse domains.

1. Introduction to Reinforcement Learning

Reinforcement learning revolves around the concept of an agent interacting with an environment, where the agent takes actions to maximize cumulative rewards over time. At each time step, the agent observes the current state of the environment, selects an action based on its policy, receives a reward, and transitions to a new state. The goal of the agent is to learn an optimal policy that maximizes expected cumulative rewards over the long run.

Agent: The decision-making entity that interacts with the environment.

Environment: The external system with which the agent interacts.

State: A representation of the current situation or configuration of the environment.

Action: The decision made by the agent to transition from one state to another.

Reward: The feedback signal provided by the environment to the agent after each action, indicating the desirability of the outcome.

Policy: The strategy or rule that governs the agent's decision-making process.

Value Function: An estimate of the expected cumulative rewards associated with being in a particular state or taking a particular action.

2. Exploration vs. Exploitation Trade-off

One of the fundamental challenges in reinforcement learning is the exploration-exploitation trade-off. The agent must balance between exploring new actions and exploiting known actions that have yielded high rewards in the past. Balancing exploration and exploitation is crucial for discovering optimal policies while maximizing cumulative rewards over time.

3. Reinforcement Learning Algorithms

Reinforcement learning algorithms can be categorized into several classes, including model-free methods, model-based methods, policy-based methods, and value-based methods. Each class of algorithms employs distinct techniques and strategies for learning optimal policies in reinforcement learning tasks.

3.1. Model-Free Methods

Model-free reinforcement learning algorithms learn directly from experience without explicitly modeling the dynamics of the environment. These algorithms estimate value functions or policies from sampled experience and improve them iteratively through trial and error. Examples of model-free methods include

Q-learning, SARSA (State-Action-Reward-State-Action), and Deep Q-Networks (DQN).

3.2. Model-Based Methods

Model-based reinforcement learning algorithms leverage explicit models of the environment's dynamics to make predictions about future states and rewards. These algorithms learn a model from observed transitions and use it to plan or simulate future trajectories. Model-based methods can improve sample efficiency and stability but require accurate models of the environment. Examples include Monte Carlo Tree Search (MCTS) and Dyna-Q.

3.3. Policy-Based Methods

Policy-based reinforcement learning algorithms directly parameterize and optimize the agent's policy, bypassing the need to learn value functions explicitly. These algorithms aim to find the policy that maximizes expected cumulative rewards directly. Policy-based methods are well-suited for continuous action spaces and can learn stochastic policies. Examples include REINFORCE, Proximal Policy Optimization (PPO), and Trust Region Policy Optimization (TRPO)

3.4. Value-Based Methods

Value-based reinforcement learning algorithms estimate the value of being in a particular state or taking a particular action and use these value estimates to derive optimal policies. These algorithms learn value functions iteratively and update them based on observed rewards and transitions. Value-based methods are popular for discrete action spaces and can handle large state spaces. Examples include Q-learning, SARSA, and Deep Q-Networks (DQN).

4. Training and Evaluation in Reinforcement Learning

Training reinforcement learning agents involves iteratively interacting with the environment, observing states, taking actions, receiving rewards, and updating value functions or policies based on observed experiences. Reinforcement learning algorithms employ various training techniques and exploration strategies to learn optimal policies effectively.

4.1. Exploration Strategies

Exploration strategies play a crucial role in reinforcement learning by determining how the agent explores the environment to gather information about states and actions. Common exploration strategies include ε-greedy exploration, softmax exploration, upper confidence bound (UCB) exploration, and Thompson sampling.

4.2. Evaluation Metrics

Evaluating the performance of reinforcement learning agents involves assessing their ability to learn optimal policies that maximize cumulative rewards over time. Common evaluation metrics include cumulative rewards, average reward per episode, convergence speed, and sample efficiency. Additionally, benchmarks such as the OpenAI Gym environment provide standardized environments and evaluation protocols for comparing different reinforcement learning algorithms.

5. Applications of Reinforcement Learning

Reinforcement learning finds applications across a wide range of domains and industries, including robotics, autonomous systems, gaming, finance, healthcare, and recommendation systems. Some prominent applications include:

Robotics: Control and navigation of robotic agents in complex environments.

Gaming: Learning to play video games at human or superhuman levels.

Finance: Portfolio management, algorithmic trading, and risk management.

Healthcare: Personalized treatment planning, drug discovery, and medical image analysis.

Recommendation Systems: Content recommendation, personalized marketing, and user engagement optimization.

6. Challenges and Future Directions

Reinforcement learning faces several challenges, including sample efficiency, exploration in high-dimensional spaces, generalization to unseen environments, and safety and ethical concerns in real-world applications. Addressing these challenges requires advances in algorithmic development, computational methodologies, and interdisciplinary research efforts. Additionally, emerging trends such as meta-learning, hierarchical reinforcement learning, and multi-agent reinforcement learning offer promising avenues for future research and innovation in reinforcement learning.

reinforcement learning stands as a powerful paradigm for learning optimal decision-making policies through interaction with an environment. By balancing exploration and exploitation, reinforcement learning agents can navigate complex environments, discover optimal strategies, and achieve superhuman performance in various domains. As the field continues to evolve, reinforcement learning holds the promise of revolutionizing industries, advancing scientific research, and augmenting human capabilities in unprecedented ways.

Transfer Learning: Leveraging Knowledge Across Domains

Transfer learning stands as a pivotal technique within the domain of machine learning, focusing on the utilization of knowledge gained from one task or domain to improve performance on a different but related task or domain. Unlike traditional machine learning paradigms, which train models from scratch using task-specific data, transfer learning enables the transfer of learned representations, features, or knowledge from a source domain to a target domain, thereby reducing the need for extensive labeled data and accelerating the learning process. In this comprehensive exploration, we delve into the principles, methodologies, algorithms, and practical applications of transfer learning, elucidating its significance in knowledge transfer and adaptation across diverse domains.

1. Introduction to Transfer Learning

Transfer learning encompasses a range of techniques and methodologies aimed at leveraging knowledge acquired from one domain to enhance learning in a different domain. At its core, transfer learning recognizes that learning tasks or domains often exhibit shared underlying structures, patterns, or representations. By transferring knowledge from a source domain with abundant data or pre-trained models to a target domain with limited data or a related but different task, transfer learning enables more efficient learning and improved performance.

1.1. Motivation for Transfer Learning

The motivation for transfer learning stems from several factors:

Data Scarcity: In many real-world scenarios, acquiring labeled data for a specific task or domain can be expensive, time-consuming, or impractical. Transfer learning addresses this challenge by leveraging existing data or models from related domains to bootstrap learning in the target domain.

Task Similarity: Tasks or domains often exhibit similarities in underlying structures, features, or concepts. Transfer learning exploits these similarities to transfer knowledge learned from one task to another, thereby improving generalization and performance on the target task.

Model Initialization: Pre-trained models trained on large-scale datasets for generic tasks such as image classification or natural language processing serve as effective starting points for learning in specific domains. Transfer learning initializes models with pre-learned representations, enabling faster convergence and improved performance.

2. Types of Transfer Learning

Transfer learning can be broadly categorized into several types based on the relationship between the source and target domains and tasks:

2.1. Inductive Transfer Learning

Inductive transfer learning involves transferring knowledge from a source domain with labeled data to a target domain with unlabeled or sparsely labeled data. The goal is to leverage shared knowledge across domains to improve learning and generalization in the target domain. Inductive transfer learning techniques include feature extraction, fine-tuning, and domain adaptation.

2.2. Transductive Transfer Learning

Transductive transfer learning focuses on transferring knowledge from a labeled source domain to a related but distinct target domain with labeled data. The objective is to exploit similarities between the source and target domains to enhance performance on the target task. Transductive transfer learning techniques include instance-based methods, kernel methods, and manifold alignment.

2.3. Unsupervised Transfer Learning

Unsupervised transfer learning aims to transfer knowledge from a source domain with unlabeled data to a target domain with labeled data. By leveraging unsupervised learning techniques such as clustering, dimensionality reduction, or generative modeling, unsupervised transfer learning extracts shared representations or structures from the source domain to improve performance on the target task.

3. Transfer Learning Techniques and Algorithms

Transfer learning encompasses a diverse array of techniques and algorithms tailored to different types of transfer scenarios and learning objectives. Some prominent transfer learning techniques include:

3.1. Feature Extraction

Feature extraction involves extracting high-level representations or features from the source domain using pre-trained models or unsupervised learning techniques and transferring these features to the target domain. Common approaches include using convolutional neural networks (CNNs) pre-trained on large-scale image datasets for computer vision tasks and using word embeddings trained on large text corpora for natural language processing tasks.

3.2. Fine-Tuning

Fine-tuning entails initializing a pre-trained model with parameters learned from the source domain and fine-tuning these parameters on the target domain using labeled data. Fine-tuning allows the model to adapt its learned representations to the specific characteristics of the target domain, thereby improving performance on the target task. Fine-tuning is commonly used in transfer learning for tasks such as image classification, object detection, and sentiment analysis.

3.3. Domain Adaptation

Domain adaptation focuses on adapting representations learned from a source domain to align with the target domain while preserving task-specific information. Domain adaptation techniques aim to minimize the distributional discrepancy between the source and target domains by learning domain-invariant features or aligning feature distributions. Domain adaptation is particularly useful in scenarios where the source and target domains exhibit domain shift or covariate shift.

3.4. Multi-Task Learning

Multi-task learning enables models to learn shared representations across multiple related tasks simultaneously, leveraging the inter-task relationships to improve generalization and performance on each task. Multi-task learning can be viewed as a form of transfer learning, where knowledge learned from one task benefits learning in other related tasks. Multi-task learning is effective in scenarios where tasks share underlying structures, dependencies, or objectives.

4. Practical Applications of Transfer Learning

Transfer learning finds applications across a wide range of domains and industries, including computer vision, natural language processing, healthcare, finance, and robotics. Some prominent applications include:

Computer Vision: Object recognition, image classification, semantic segmentation, and object detection.

Natural Language Processing: Text classification, sentiment analysis, machine translation, and named entity recognition.

Healthcare: Medical image analysis, disease diagnosis, and patient outcome prediction.

Finance: Fraud detection, credit scoring, and algorithmic trading.

Robotics: Robot navigation, manipulation, and object grasping.

5. Challenges and Considerations in Transfer Learning

While transfer learning offers numerous benefits, it also presents several challenges and considerations:

Domain Shift: Differences in the underlying distributions or characteristics between the source and target domains can hinder transfer learning performance.

Task Misalignment: Mismatches in task objectives or assumptions between the source and target tasks may limit the effectiveness of transfer learning techniques.

Data Bias: Biases present in the source domain data may propagate to the target domain, leading to biased predictions or decisions.

Model Capacity: The capacity of the transfer learning model may influence its ability to capture and transfer relevant knowledge across domains effectively.

Addressing these challenges requires careful consideration of the transfer scenario, domain characteristics, and learning objectives, as well as the selection of appropriate transfer learning techniques and evaluation methodologies.

6. Future Directions in Transfer Learning

As transfer learning continues to evolve, several future directions and research avenues emerge:

Domain-General Representations: Developing domain-general representations that capture high-level, abstract concepts and features shared across diverse domains.

Adaptive Transfer Learning: Designing adaptive transfer learning techniques that dynamically adjust to changing environments or task conditions.

Extending transfer learning to scenarios with limited labeled data or novel tasks, such as zero-shot learning and few-shot learning.

Meta-Learning: Leveraging meta-learning techniques to learn transferable knowledge and adaptation strategies across multiple transfer scenarios or tasks.

By addressing these future directions, transfer learning has the potential to further enhance learning efficiency, generalization capabilities, and adaptability across a wide range of domains and applications.

transfer learning stands as a versatile and powerful technique for leveraging knowledge across domains, tasks, and datasets to enhance learning efficiency, generalization capabilities, and performance in machine learning applications.

Chapter 5
The Ethics of AI: Challenges and Dilemmas

The rapid advancement of artificial intelligence (AI) technologies has ushered in a new era of innovation, promising transformative solutions to complex problems across various domains. However, alongside its potential benefits, AI also presents a myriad of ethical challenges and dilemmas that warrant careful consideration and proactive mitigation. In this chapter, we delve into the intricate landscape of AI ethics, exploring the ethical principles, dilemmas, and societal implications associated with the development, deployment, and impact of AI systems.

1. The Ethical Imperative

As AI technologies permeate diverse facets of society, from healthcare and finance to transportation and governance, ethical considerations become paramount. Ethical frameworks such as fairness, accountability, transparency, privacy, and security serve as guiding principles to ensure that AI systems uphold fundamental human values and rights. Balancing innovation and ethical responsibility is essential to foster trust, mitigate harms, and promote equitable outcomes in the deployment of AI technologies.

2. Ethical Dilemmas in AI

AI introduces a host of ethical dilemmas and challenges that encompass issues such as bias and fairness, interpretability and explainability, autonomy and accountability, privacy and data protection, and societal impact. Addressing these dilemmas requires interdisciplinary collaboration, ethical reasoning, and stakeholder engagement to navigate the complex interplay between technological capabilities, societal values, and legal frameworks.

3. Bias and Fairness

AI systems can perpetuate or exacerbate biases present in training data, leading to discriminatory outcomes and inequitable treatment. Mitigating bias and ensuring fairness in AI requires proactive measures such as dataset curation, algorithmic transparency, and fairness-aware model development to promote equity and mitigate harm, particularly in high-stakes domains such as criminal justice, hiring, and lending.

4. Interpretability and Explainability

The opacity of AI algorithms poses challenges to understanding their decision-making processes, raising concerns about accountability, trust, and human oversight. Enhancing the interpretability and explainability of AI systems through techniques such as model transparency, post-hoc explanation methods, and human-AI collaboration fosters trust, enables accountability, and facilitates user comprehension and acceptance.

5. Autonomy and Accountability

AI systems endowed with decision-making autonomy raise questions about accountability, responsibility, and liability in the event of errors, accidents, or unintended consequences. Establishing clear lines of responsibility, robust governance mechanisms, and legal frameworks that delineate accountability for AI-related harms is essential to uphold ethical standards, ensure recourse for affected parties, and promote trust in AI systems.

6. Privacy and Data Protection

AI's reliance on vast amounts of personal data raises concerns about privacy infringement, data misuse, and surveillance, necessitating robust data protection regulations, privacy-preserving technologies, and ethical data practices. Safeguarding individuals' privacy rights and autonomy while harnessing the benefits of AI requires a delicate balance between data utility and privacy preservation, grounded in ethical principles of consent, transparency, and accountability.

7. Societal Impact

The pervasive influence of AI technologies on society encompasses economic displacement, job automation, algorithmic governance, and socio-political polarization, posing profound ethical challenges and societal implications. Addressing these challenges requires holistic approaches that prioritize human well-being, social equity, and democratic values, fostering inclusive dialogue, policy deliberation, and ethical foresight to navigate the complex interplay between technological innovation and societal transformation.

In navigating the ethical terrain of AI, it is imperative to uphold principles of beneficence, non-maleficence, autonomy, justice, and respect for human dignity, ensuring that AI technologies serve the common good, uphold human rights, and contribute to a more equitable and sustainable future. By confronting ethical challenges head-on, fostering interdisciplinary collaboration, and promoting ethical leadership, we can harness the transformative potential of AI while safeguarding against its ethical pitfalls, thereby advancing responsible innovation and societal progress.

Bias and Fairness in AI Systems: Mitigating Discrimination and Promoting Equity

In recent years, the proliferation of artificial intelligence (AI) technologies has raised concerns about the potential for bias and unfairness in algorithmic decision-making. While AI systems hold immense promise for enhancing efficiency and accuracy across various domains, they also have the capacity to perpetuate or exacerbate societal biases present in training data, leading to discriminatory outcomes and inequitable treatment. In this detailed exploration, we delve into the complex landscape of bias and fairness in AI systems, examining the sources of bias, the challenges in addressing fairness, and the strategies for mitigating discrimination and promoting equity.

1. Understanding Bias in AI Systems

Bias in AI systems refers to systematic errors or unfairness in decision-making processes that result from the encoding or amplification of societal biases present in training data, algorithmic design, or deployment contexts. Bias can manifest in various forms, including demographic bias, cultural bias, cognitive bias, and historical bias, and can impact outcomes across a wide range of domains, including criminal justice, healthcare, hiring, lending, and advertising.

1.1. Sources of Bias

Training Data Bias: Biases present in training data, such as underrepresentation or overrepresentation of certain demographic groups, can lead to skewed model predictions and discriminatory outcomes.

Algorithmic Bias: Biases inherent in algorithmic design, such as feature selection, model architecture, or optimization objectives, can perpetuate or amplify existing societal biases present in training data.

Deployment Bias: Biases introduced during the deployment or operationalization of AI systems, such as biased feedback loops, unequal access to resources, or differential treatment of user groups, can exacerbate fairness concerns and contribute to disparate impacts on marginalized communities.

1.2. Types of Bias

Demographic Bias: Bias based on demographic characteristics such as race, gender, age, or socioeconomic status, leading to differential treatment or outcomes for different demographic groups.

Cultural Bias: Bias stemming from cultural norms, values, or perspectives encoded in training data or reflected in algorithmic decision-making, resulting in unfair treatment or misrepresentation of cultural minorities.

Cognitive Bias: Bias arising from cognitive heuristics or decision-making shortcuts embedded in AI algorithms, leading to systematic errors or distortions in judgment.

Historical Bias: Bias inherited from historical injustices, inequalities, or discriminatory practices encoded in societal structures and reflected in training data, perpetuating intergenerational cycles of disadvantage and marginalization.

2. Challenges in Addressing Fairness

Addressing fairness in AI systems poses numerous challenges, stemming from the inherent complexity of algorithmic decision-making, the multidimensional nature of bias, and the dynamic socio-technical contexts in which AI operates. Some key challenges include:

2.1. Measurement and Definition of Fairness:

Defining and operationalizing fairness in AI systems is inherently subjective and context-dependent, requiring careful consideration of ethical principles, stakeholder perspectives, and societal values. Different fairness metrics, such as demographic parity, equal opportunity, and disparate impact, may prioritize different aspects of fairness and lead to trade-offs between competing objectives.

2.2. Trade-offs between Fairness and Accuracy:

Striking a balance between fairness and accuracy poses a fundamental trade-off in algorithmic decision-making. Mitigating bias to achieve fairness may come at the expense of predictive performance or utility, raising questions about the optimal allocation of resources and the acceptable level of risk or error in decision-making processes.

2.3. Intersectionality and Multiple Biases:

Individuals may belong to multiple overlapping demographic groups and experience intersecting forms of bias, complicating efforts to address fairness comprehensively. Intersectional approaches to fairness recognize the interconnected nature of social identities and aim to account for the unique experiences and vulnerabilities of marginalized communities.

2.4. Feedback Loops and Systemic Bias:

Biases perpetuated by AI systems can create feedback loops that reinforce existing disparities and exacerbate social inequalities over time. Addressing systemic bias requires systemic interventions that address root causes, challenge structural inequalities, and promote systemic change across institutions and socio-technical ecosystems.

3. Mitigating Bias and Promoting Fairness

Despite the challenges, there are several strategies and best practices for mitigating bias and promoting fairness in AI systems:

3.1. Data Collection and Curation:

Ensuring representative and diverse training data that captures the full spectrum of human diversity and avoids reinforcing existing biases is essential for mitigating bias at the source. Data collection methods should be transparent, inclusive, and accountable, with mechanisms for identifying and correcting bias in training data.

3.2. Algorithmic Fairness Techniques: Employing algorithmic fairness techniques such as fairness-aware machine learning, bias detection and mitigation algorithms, and fairness constraints or regularizers can help mitigate bias and promote fairness in AI systems. These techniques aim to identify, quantify, and mitigate biases at different stages of the machine learning pipeline, from data preprocessing to model training and deployment.

3.3. Interpretability and Explainability:

Enhancing the interpretability and explainability of AI systems can help uncover hidden biases, enable stakeholders to understand the rationale behind algorithmic decisions, and facilitate accountability and recourse for individuals affected by biased outcomes. Explainable AI techniques such as interpretable models, model-agnostic explanation methods, and causal inference approaches can shed light on the factors driving algorithmic decisions and uncover instances of bias or discrimination.

3.4. Human-in-the-Loop Approaches:

Integrating human oversight, feedback, and intervention into AI systems through human-in-the-loop approaches can provide checks and balances against algorithmic biases, ensure alignment with ethical principles and societal norms, and promote accountability and transparency in decision-making processes. Human-in-the-loop systems empower individuals to challenge biased decisions, correct errors, and provide context-specific insights that may not be captured by algorithms alone.

3.5. Diversity and Inclusion in AI Development:

Promoting diversity and inclusion in AI research, development, and deployment is essential for mitigating bias and promoting fairness. Diverse teams bring a range of perspectives, experiences, and expertise to the design and implementation of AI systems, helping to identify and address biases that may otherwise go unnoticed. Inclusive design practices prioritize the needs and preferences of diverse user groups and ensure that AI systems are accessible, equitable, and responsive to the needs of all stakeholders.

bias and fairness in AI systems represent complex and multifaceted challenges that require careful consideration, proactive intervention, and collaborative efforts across disciplines and stakeholders. By understanding the sources and manifestations of bias, acknowledging the challenges in addressing fairness, and adopting strategies for mitigating bias and promoting fairness, we can work towards the development of AI systems that uphold ethical principles, respect human dignity, and contribute to a more just and equitable society. Through continued research, innovation, and engagement, we can harness the transformative potential of AI while mitigating its risks and ensuring that it serves the common good.

Privacy Concerns in the Age of Big Data: Safeguarding Personal Information in a Digital World

In the era of Big Data, where vast amounts of information are generated, collected, and analyzed at unprecedented scales, privacy concerns have become increasingly prevalent and complex. The widespread adoption of digital technologies, the proliferation of online services, and the interconnectedness of digital ecosystems have ushered in new challenges and risks to individual privacy rights and personal data protection. In this comprehensive exploration, we delve into the multifaceted landscape of privacy concerns in the age of Big Data, examining the sources of privacy risks, the implications for individuals and society, and the strategies for safeguarding personal information in a digital world.

1. Understanding Privacy in the Digital Age

Privacy, in the context of the digital age, encompasses the right of individuals to control their personal information, maintain autonomy over their digital identities, and preserve confidentiality in their online interactions. It encompasses various dimensions, including informational privacy (the control over personal data), decisional privacy (the freedom to make choices without interference), and spatial privacy (the right to privacy in physical and virtual spaces). In the age of Big Data, privacy concerns extend beyond traditional notions of data protection to encompass issues such as surveillance, profiling, data breaches, and algorithmic discrimination.

2. Sources of Privacy Risks in Big Data

The emergence of Big Data technologies has introduced several sources of privacy risks and vulnerabilities:

2.1. Data Collection Practices:

The pervasive collection of personal data by online platforms, IoT devices, mobile apps, and sensors raises concerns about the scope, granularity, and purpose of data collection. The aggregation and linkage of disparate datasets can lead to the creation of comprehensive profiles that intrude upon individuals' privacy and enable sophisticated forms of surveillance and targeting.

2.2. Data Processing and Analysis:

The processing and analysis of Big Data using advanced analytics techniques such as machine learning, AI, and data mining pose risks to privacy due to the potential for algorithmic inference, re-identification, and unintended disclosures. Algorithmic decision-making based on predictive models derived from Big Data can result in discriminatory outcomes, privacy violations, and loss of individual autonomy.

2.3. Data Sharing and Third-party Access:

The sharing of personal data among organizations, data brokers, advertisers, and third-party service providers introduces risks of unauthorized access, data breaches, and data misuse. Lack of transparency, consent, and accountability in data sharing practices can undermine individuals' control over their personal information and erode trust in digital platforms and services.

2.4. Surveillance and Monitoring:

The proliferation of surveillance technologies, including CCTV cameras, facial recognition systems, and location tracking tools, enables pervasive monitoring of individuals' activities, behaviors, and movements. Mass surveillance programs by governments and corporations raise concerns about privacy infringements, civil liberties, and the chilling effects on free expression and dissent.

3. Implications of Privacy Concerns

Privacy concerns in the age of Big Data have profound implications for individuals, organizations, and society as a whole:

3.1. Individual Autonomy and Freedom:

Privacy violations erode individuals' autonomy and freedom to control their personal information, make independent choices, and express themselves without fear of surveillance or interference. Loss of privacy can lead to self-censorship, social conformity, and diminished trust in digital technologies and institutions.

3.2. Trust and Transparency:

Privacy breaches undermine trust in organizations, governments, and digital platforms, eroding confidence in their ability to protect personal data and uphold privacy rights. Lack of transparency in data practices, data sharing agreements, and algorithmic decision-making exacerbates distrust and skepticism among users and stakeholders.

3.3. Data Security and Trustworthiness:

Privacy risks pose threats to data security, integrity, and confidentiality, increasing the likelihood of data breaches, identity theft, and fraud. Data breaches not only result in financial losses and reputational damage but also erode public trust in the security and trustworthiness of digital systems and services.

3.4. Social Justice and Equity: Privacy infringements

disproportionately impact marginalized communities, exacerbating existing inequalities and vulnerabilities. Biases in data collection, algorithmic decision-making, and surveillance practices can perpetuate discrimination, amplify social disparities, and undermine efforts to promote social justice and equity in society.

4. Strategies for Safeguarding Personal Information

Addressing privacy concerns in the age of Big Data requires a multifaceted approach that combines technological, regulatory, and societal interventions:

4.1. Data Minimization and Anonymization:

Adopting data minimization practices to limit the collection, retention, and processing of personal data to what is necessary for specific purposes can reduce privacy risks. Anonymization techniques such as differential privacy, k-anonymity, and data masking can help protect individual privacy while enabling data analysis and sharing for legitimate purposes.

4.2. Privacy by Design and Default:

Integrating privacy considerations into the design and development of digital systems and services, known as privacy by design and default, ensures that privacy protections are built-in from the outset. Principles such as data protection, user consent, transparency, and user control should guide the design of privacy-preserving technologies and practices.

4.3. Enhanced Transparency and Accountability:

Promoting transparency and accountability in data practices, data governance, and algorithmic decision-making fosters trust and confidence among users and stakeholders. Organizations should provide clear and accessible information about their data practices, data sharing agreements, and privacy policies, enabling users to make informed choices and exercise control over their personal information.

4.4. Regulatory Frameworks and Legal Protections:

Strengthening regulatory frameworks and legal protections for personal data, such as the General Data Protection Regulation (GDPR) in the European Union and the California Consumer Privacy Act (CCPA) in the United States, provides legal safeguards and enforcement mechanisms to protect individuals' privacy rights. Governments, policymakers, and regulatory bodies play a critical role in establishing and enforcing privacy regulations that hold organizations accountable for privacy violations and empower individuals to assert their privacy rights.

4.5. Empowering Users and Civil Society:

Empowering users with knowledge, tools, and resources to protect their privacy rights and advocate for privacy-enhancing technologies and practices is essential for promoting a culture of privacy-consciousness and digital literacy. Civil society organizations, privacy advocates, and consumer rights groups play a crucial role in raising awareness, advocating for privacy rights, and holding organizations and governments accountable for privacy infringements.

Privacy concerns in the age of Big Data pose significant challenges and risks to individual privacy rights, autonomy, and trust in digital systems and services. By understanding the sources and implications of privacy risks, adopting privacy-enhancing technologies and practices, and strengthening regulatory protections and legal safeguards, we can mitigate privacy concerns, promote responsible data stewardship, and uphold privacy rights in a digital world. Through collective efforts and collaboration among stakeholders, we can navigate the complexities of privacy in the age of Big Data while harnessing the transformative potential of data-driven innovation for the benefit of society as a whole.

Autonomous Weapons: The Moral Debate

The development and deployment of autonomous weapons systems have sparked intense moral debates worldwide. These systems, capable of identifying and engaging targets without direct human intervention, raise profound ethical questions about the nature of warfare, human responsibility, and the preservation of fundamental moral principles. In this detailed exploration, we delve into the moral debate surrounding autonomous weapons, examining the arguments for and against their use, the ethical concerns they raise, and the implications for international law and global security.

1. Understanding Autonomous Weapons

Autonomous weapons, also known as lethal autonomous weapons systems (LAWS) or killer robots, are weapons systems that can independently select and engage targets without human intervention. These systems utilize artificial intelligence (AI), machine learning algorithms, and sensor technologies to identify, track, and neutralize targets based on predefined criteria or decision-making algorithms. Unlike traditional weapons systems, which require human operators to authorize and execute lethal actions, autonomous weapons operate autonomously, raising concerns about accountability, control, and ethical decision-making in warfare.

2. Arguments for the Use of Autonomous Weapons

Proponents of autonomous weapons argue that these systems offer several potential advantages in military operations:

2.1. Operational Efficiency:

Autonomous weapons have the potential to enhance operational efficiency by enabling faster decision-making, reducing response times, and improving tactical effectiveness on the battlefield. These systems can analyze vast amounts of data, assess situational dynamics, and execute precise actions with greater speed and accuracy than human operators, potentially gaining a strategic advantage in combat scenarios.

2.2. Risk Reduction for Military Personnel:

By delegating dangerous or high-risk tasks to autonomous systems, military personnel can be spared from exposure to harm or hazardous environments, reducing casualties and preserving human lives on the battlefield. Autonomous weapons can undertake missions in hostile or inhospitable conditions, operate in contested environments, and execute missions with minimal risk to human operators.

2.3. Enhanced Target Discrimination and Precision:

Autonomous weapons systems equipped with advanced sensor technologies and AI algorithms can theoretically improve target discrimination and precision, minimizing collateral damage and civilian casualties in military operations. These systems can analyze sensor data in real-time, distinguish between combatants and non-combatants, and engage targets with greater accuracy and discrimination than human operators under stressful or time-critical conditions.

2.4. Strategic Deterrence and Defense:

The development and deployment of autonomous weapons can serve as a deterrent against potential adversaries, enhancing deterrence capabilities and strengthening national defense postures. Autonomous systems can be deployed for strategic reconnaissance, surveillance, and deterrence missions, deterring aggression, and enhancing situational awareness in contested regions or conflict zones.

3. Ethical Concerns and Moral Implications

Despite the potential advantages, autonomous weapons raise profound ethical concerns and moral implications:

3.1. Lack of Human Control and Accountability:

The autonomous nature of these weapons systems raises questions about human control, responsibility, and accountability in the decision to employ lethal force. Unlike human operators who can exercise judgment, empathy, and ethical reasoning, autonomous weapons lack the capacity for moral agency and cannot be held accountable for their actions, leading to concerns about the delegation of life-and-death decisions to machines.

3.2. Violation of Human Dignity and Rights:

The deployment of autonomous weapons in warfare poses risks to human dignity, rights, and the principles of proportionality and distinction in armed conflict. These systems may lack the ability to discriminate between combatants and non-combatants, adhere to rules of engagement, or exercise restraint in the use of force, potentially leading to indiscriminate or disproportionate attacks that violate international humanitarian law and human rights principles.

3.3. Potential for Unintended Consequences and Escalation:

The use of autonomous weapons introduces risks of unintended consequences, misinterpretations, and escalation in conflict situations. These systems may malfunction, misidentify targets, or respond unpredictably to dynamic and complex environments, leading to unintended harm, civilian casualties, and escalation of hostilities. Moreover, the deployment of autonomous weapons could lower the threshold for the use of force, increase the likelihood of conflicts, and undermine diplomatic efforts to resolve disputes peacefully.

3.4. Arms Race and Proliferation Concerns:

The development and deployment of autonomous weapons could fuel an arms race among nations, leading to the proliferation of advanced military technologies and the erosion of strategic stability. The pursuit of autonomous weapons by state and non-state actors could trigger a proliferation cascade, exacerbate regional tensions, and undermine efforts to control the spread of weapons of mass destruction (WMDs) and conventional arms.

4. International Law and Regulatory Challenges

The ethical debate surrounding autonomous weapons intersects with legal and regulatory challenges under international humanitarian law (IHL) and arms control regimes:

4.1. Compliance with International Humanitarian Law:

The use of autonomous weapons must comply with the principles of distinction, proportionality, and precaution under IHL, which regulate the conduct of armed conflict and aim to minimize harm to civilians and non-combatants. Autonomous weapons must be capable of distinguishing between lawful and unlawful targets, adhering to rules of engagement, and minimizing collateral damage in accordance with IHL standards.

4.2. Regulatory Frameworks and Arms Control: Efforts to regulate autonomous weapons and prevent their indiscriminate or unethical use have led to calls for international agreements, treaties, and arms control regimes to govern their development, deployment, and use. Proposals for a preemptive ban, moratorium, or regulatory framework for autonomous weapons seek to establish norms, standards, and safeguards to mitigate ethical risks and prevent destabilizing consequences in warfare.

4.3. Challenges of Enforcement and Verification:

Implementing and enforcing regulatory measures for autonomous weapons pose challenges related to verification, monitoring, and compliance verification. Autonomous systems may lack transparency, auditability, or accountability mechanisms, making it difficult to assess their compliance with legal and ethical standards and verify their adherence to regulatory requirements.

The moral debate surrounding autonomous weapons raises fundamental questions about the nature of warfare, human agency, and ethical responsibility in the use of lethal force. While proponents argue for the operational advantages and strategic benefits of autonomous weapons, critics raise concerns about the lack of human control, ethical risks, and legal implications of delegating life-and-death decisions to machines. As the development and deployment of autonomous weapons continue to evolve, it is essential to engage in an informed and inclusive dialogue, uphold ethical principles, and establish robust legal and regulatory frameworks to safeguard against the ethical risks and moral pitfalls of autonomous warfare. Through concerted efforts and international cooperation, we can navigate the moral complexities of autonomous weapons and ensure that advances in technology serve the cause of peace, justice, and human dignity in the modern battlefield.

AI and Employment: Addressing Job Displacement

The rapid advancement of artificial intelligence (AI) technologies has led to growing concerns about the potential for job displacement and disruption across various industries. As AI systems become increasingly capable of automating tasks traditionally performed by humans, workers face the prospect of job loss, skill obsolescence, and economic dislocation. In this comprehensive exploration, we delve into the complex relationship between AI and employment, examining the drivers of job displacement, the potential impacts on the workforce, and the strategies for addressing the challenges of AI-induced automation.

1. Understanding AI-induced Job Displacement

AI-induced job displacement refers to the phenomenon whereby AI technologies automate tasks, roles, or occupations traditionally performed by humans, leading to changes in employment patterns, workforce composition, and skill requirements. The automation of routine, repetitive, and predictable tasks using AI algorithms, machine learning, and robotic technologies has the potential to transform the nature of work, reshape industries, and disrupt labor markets.

1.1. Drivers of Job Displacement

Several factors contribute to AI-induced job displacement:

Advancements in AI Technologies: Rapid advancements in AI technologies, including machine learning, natural language processing, computer vision, and robotics, enable the automation of an increasing range of tasks across diverse sectors, from manufacturing and transportation to healthcare and finance.

Cost Savings and Efficiency Gains: Employers are motivated to adopt AI technologies to achieve cost savings, improve productivity, and enhance operational efficiency by replacing human labor with automated systems that can perform tasks faster, cheaper, and with greater precision.

Globalization and Outsourcing: AI-induced automation amplifies the pressures of globalization and outsourcing, as companies seek to remain competitive in a globalized economy by outsourcing labor-intensive tasks to lower-cost regions or replacing domestic workers with AI-powered solutions.

Changing Nature of Work: The nature of work is evolving due to technological advancements, demographic shifts, and changing consumer preferences, leading to the emergence of new job roles, skill requirements, and employment opportunities in sectors such as digital technology, data analytics, and creative industries.

1.2. Potential Impacts on the Workforce

AI-induced job displacement can have various impacts on the workforce:

Job Losses: Workers in occupations susceptible to automation, such as routine manual tasks, administrative functions, and repetitive assembly-line work, may face job losses or displacement as AI technologies automate these tasks more efficiently and cost-effectively.

Skill Obsolescence: Workers whose skills are rendered obsolete by AI-induced automation may experience difficulty transitioning to new roles or industries that require different skill sets, leading to unemployment, underemployment, or precarious employment.

Income Inequality: AI-induced automation may exacerbate income inequality by disproportionately displacing low-skilled workers in routine, manual jobs while creating new opportunities and high-paying roles for highly-skilled professionals with specialized technical skills and expertise in AI-related fields.

Labor Market Polarization: AI-induced automation can contribute to labor market polarization, with job growth concentrated at the high end (e.g., knowledge workers, professionals) and low end (e.g., service workers, gig economy) of the skill spectrum, while middle-skilled jobs (e.g., clerical, manufacturing) experience decline or stagnation.

2. Strategies for Addressing AI-induced Job Displacement

Addressing the challenges of AI-induced job displacement requires a multi-faceted approach that encompasses technological, economic, and social interventions:

2.1. Upskilling and Reskilling

Investing in education and training programs to upskill and reskill the workforce for the jobs of the future is essential for mitigating the impacts of AI-induced automation. Training initiatives should focus on developing skills that are in high demand in emerging industries such as data science, artificial intelligence, cybersecurity, and digital marketing, as well as fostering adaptability, critical thinking, and problem-solving abilities that are transferrable across occupations.

2.2. Lifelong Learning and Continuous Education

Promoting a culture of lifelong learning and continuous education is essential for equipping workers with the skills and knowledge needed to thrive in a rapidly evolving labor market. Governments, employers, and educational institutions should collaborate to provide accessible, affordable, and flexible learning opportunities that enable individuals to acquire new skills, update existing competencies, and adapt to changing job requirements throughout their careers.

2.3. Talent Development and Talent Mobility

Facilitating talent development and talent mobility across industries and sectors can help match workers with job opportunities that align with their skills, interests, and aspirations. Initiatives such as career counseling, job matching platforms, apprenticeship programs, and internships can facilitate transitions between occupations and industries, reduce frictional unemployment, and promote economic resilience in the face of technological change.

2.4. Social Safety Nets and Economic Support

Enhancing social safety nets and economic support mechanisms is essential for protecting workers adversely affected by AI-induced job displacement. Policies such as unemployment insurance, job retraining grants, wage subsidies, and income support programs can provide temporary assistance to displaced workers, alleviate financial hardship, and facilitate transitions to new employment opportunities.

2.5. Inclusive Growth and Economic Development

Fostering inclusive growth and economic development is critical for ensuring that the benefits of AI-induced automation are equitably distributed across society. Governments, businesses, and civil society organizations should collaborate to create inclusive economic policies, promote equitable access to education and training, and invest in infrastructure, innovation, and entrepreneurship to create new job opportunities and stimulate economic growth in underserved communities.

2.6. Ethical Considerations and Human-Centered AI

Embedding ethical considerations and human-centered principles into the design, development, and deployment of AI technologies is essential for mitigating the negative impacts of AI-induced automation on the workforce. Ethical AI frameworks should prioritize fairness, transparency, accountability, and inclusivity to ensure that AI systems enhance human capabilities, augment human judgment, and promote human well-being while minimizing adverse consequences for workers and society.

AI-induced job displacement presents significant challenges and opportunities for the future of work, requiring proactive measures and collaborative efforts to mitigate its negative impacts and harness its potential benefits. By investing in education and training, promoting lifelong learning and continuous education, facilitating talent development and mobility, strengthening social safety nets and economic support mechanisms, fostering inclusive growth and economic development, and embedding ethical considerations into AI development, we can navigate the complexities of AI-induced automation and ensure that technological advancements contribute to shared prosperity, sustainable development, and human flourishing in the 21st century workforce. Through collective action and innovation, we can build a future where AI augments human capabilities, creates new opportunities, and fosters inclusive growth for all.

Chapter 6
Natural Language Processing: Deciphering Human Speec

Natural Language Processing (NLP) is a field of artificial intelligence (AI) that focuses on the interaction between computers and human language. It encompasses a range of techniques and methodologies aimed at understanding, interpreting, and generating human speech and text data. In an era characterized by the proliferation of digital content, social media, and conversational interfaces, NLP plays a vital role in enabling machines to comprehend and respond to human language in a manner that is both contextually relevant and semantically accurate.

At its core, NLP seeks to bridge the gap between human communication and machine understanding, enabling computers to decipher the complexities of human speech, including nuances in semantics, syntax, and pragmatics. From speech recognition and machine translation to sentiment analysis and chatbots, NLP applications span a diverse array of domains and industries, revolutionizing the way we interact with technology and transforming the landscape of human-computer interaction.

In this exploration of NLP, we delve into the fundamental principles, methodologies, and applications that underpin the field, examining the challenges and opportunities of deciphering human speech and harnessing the power of natural language understanding in the digital age. Through a comprehensive examination of NLP techniques, we seek to unravel the mysteries of human language and unlock the transformative potential of AI-driven communication.

Tokenization and Text Preprocessing: Enhancing Natural Language Processing

Tokenization and text preprocessing are fundamental techniques in natural language processing (NLP) that involve breaking down raw text data into smaller, more manageable units and preparing it for further analysis. These preprocessing steps play a crucial role in tasks such as text classification, sentiment analysis, machine translation, and information retrieval by transforming unstructured text data into structured representations that can be processed by machine learning algorithms. In this comprehensive exploration, we delve into the concepts of tokenization and text preprocessing, examining their importance, common techniques, and best practices for enhancing NLP tasks.

1. Introduction to Tokenization and Text Preprocessing

Tokenization is the process of splitting raw text data into smaller units called tokens, which can be words, subwords, characters, or symbols. Text preprocessing, on the other hand, encompasses a broader set of techniques aimed at cleaning, normalizing, and transforming text data to make it suitable for NLP tasks. These preprocessing steps typically include tokenization, lowercasing, removing punctuation, stopwords, and special characters, stemming or lemmatization, and handling numerical data, URLs, and emojis.

2. Importance of Tokenization and Text Preprocessing

Tokenization and text preprocessing are essential for several reasons:

Normalization: Tokenization and preprocessing help standardize the format and representation of text data by removing irregularities, inconsistencies, and noise, making it easier to analyze and interpret.

Dimensionality Reduction: By breaking down text data into smaller units (tokens), tokenization reduces the dimensionality of the input space, making it more manageable for machine learning algorithms and reducing computational complexity.

Feature Extraction: Preprocessing techniques such as stemming, lemmatization, and removal of stopwords and punctuation help extract meaningful features from text data, capturing the underlying semantics and reducing the influence of irrelevant or redundant information.

Improving Model Performance: Clean, normalized text data obtained through tokenization and preprocessing can improve the performance of NLP models by reducing overfitting, improving generalization, and enhancing the interpretability of model predictions.

3. Common Techniques in Tokenization and Text Preprocessing

Several techniques are commonly used in tokenization and text preprocessing:

3.1. Tokenization

Word Tokenization: Breaking text into words based on whitespace or punctuation boundaries. For example, "The quick brown fox" would be tokenized into ["The", "quick", "brown", "fox"].

Sentence Tokenization: Splitting text into sentences based on punctuation cues such as periods, exclamation marks, or question marks. For example, "Hello! How are you?" would be tokenized into ["Hello!", "How are you?"].

Subword Tokenization: Decomposing words into smaller subword units to handle out-of-vocabulary words and improve the coverage of language models. Techniques such as Byte-Pair Encoding (BPE), WordPiece, and SentencePiece are commonly used for subword tokenization.

3.2. Text Preprocessing

Lowercasing: Converting all text to lowercase to standardize the representation of words and reduce vocabulary size. For example, "Hello" and "hello" would be treated as the same token.

Removing Punctuation: Eliminating punctuation marks from text data to focus on the semantic content of the text and reduce noise. For example, removing periods, commas, and quotation marks.

Removing Stopwords: Filtering out common stopwords such as "the", "is", "and" that carry little semantic meaning and may introduce noise into the analysis. Stopwords lists are available for various languages and can be customized based on the specific task or domain.

Stemming and Lemmatization: Normalizing words to their root forms to reduce inflectional variations and improve feature extraction. Stemming removes suffixes to obtain the stem of a word (e.g., "running" becomes "run"), while lemmatization maps words to their base or dictionary form (e.g., "ran" becomes "run").

Handling Numerical Data and Special Characters: Treating numerical data, URLs, emojis, and other special characters appropriately by replacing them with placeholders, removing them, or encoding them in a standardized format.

4. Best Practices for Tokenization and Text Preprocessing

Effective tokenization and text preprocessing require careful consideration of several factors and best practices:

Language and Domain-Specific Processing: Tokenization and preprocessing techniques should be tailored to the specific language and domain of the text data to capture linguistic nuances, domain-specific vocabulary, and cultural context effectively.

Data Cleaning and Quality Assurance: Prioritize data cleaning and quality assurance to identify and address errors, inconsistencies, and outliers in the text data before preprocessing. This may involve spell checking, typo correction, and manual inspection of the data for accuracy and relevance.

Evaluation and Iteration: Evaluate the impact of tokenization and preprocessing techniques on downstream NLP tasks such as classification, clustering, or sentiment analysis, and iterate on the preprocessing pipeline based on empirical performance metrics and domain expertise.

Balancing Flexibility and Standardization: Balance the need for flexibility and customization with the benefits of standardization and reproducibility in tokenization and preprocessing pipelines. Adopt modular, configurable preprocessing workflows that can be easily adapted to different datasets and tasks while maintaining consistency and coherence in the preprocessing steps.

Tokenization and text preprocessing are foundational techniques in NLP that play a crucial role in transforming raw text data into structured representations suitable for machine learning algorithms. By breaking down text into smaller units (tokens) and applying preprocessing techniques such as lowercasing, removing punctuation, stopwords, and stemming, we can extract meaningful features, reduce noise, and improve the performance of NLP models. Effective tokenization and preprocessing require careful consideration of language-specific characteristics, domain-specific requirements, and best practices for data cleaning, quality assurance, and evaluation. By adopting standardized preprocessing pipelines, leveraging domain expertise, and iteratively refining preprocessing workflows based on empirical performance, we can enhance the effectiveness and robustness of NLP applications across diverse domains and languages. Through continued research, innovation, and collaboration, we can advance the state-of-the-art in tokenization and text preprocessing and unlock new possibilities for extracting knowledge and insights from unstructured text data in the era of big data and artificial intelligence.

Word Embeddings: Capturing Semantic Meaning

Word embeddings are a fundamental technique in natural language processing (NLP) that aim to capture the semantic meaning of words by representing them as dense, low-dimensional vectors in a continuous vector space. This transformative approach to word representation has revolutionized various NLP tasks, including language modeling, text classification, sentiment analysis, and machine translation. In this comprehensive exploration, we delve into the concept of word embeddings, examining their importance, underlying methodologies, and applications in capturing semantic meaning in textual data.

1. Introduction to Word Embeddings

Word embeddings are dense vector representations of words in a continuous vector space, where words with similar meanings are represented by vectors that are close together in the space. Unlike traditional approaches to word representation, such as one-hot encoding or bag-of-words models, which result in high-dimensional and sparse representations, word embeddings encode semantic relationships between words in a compact and distributed manner.

2. Importance of Word Embeddings

Word embeddings are crucial for several reasons:

Semantic Representation: Word embeddings capture semantic relationships between words by placing them in a continuous vector space, where similarity between vectors corresponds to semantic similarity between words. This enables algorithms to capture subtle nuances in meaning, context, and usage, facilitating more accurate and contextually relevant language understanding.

Dimensionality Reduction: Word embeddings reduce the dimensionality of the word space by representing words as dense vectors of fixed length, enabling more efficient computation and storage compared to high-dimensional, sparse representations such as one-hot encoding or bag-of-words models.

Generalization: Word embeddings generalize across words and contexts by learning distributed representations that capture common semantic features shared by words with similar meanings or usage patterns. This enables models to handle out-of-vocabulary words, rare terms, and unseen contexts more effectively, enhancing their robustness and adaptability.

3. Methodologies for Generating Word Embeddings

Several methodologies are commonly used to generate word embeddings:

Word2Vec: Word2Vec is a popular method for learning word embeddings based on a shallow neural network architecture known as continuous bag-of-words (CBOW) or skip-gram. Word2Vec models predict the context words surrounding a target word within a fixed-size context window, learning distributed representations that capture semantic similarities between words.

GloVe (Global Vectors for Word Representation): GloVe is an unsupervised learning algorithm for generating word embeddings by factorizing the word co-occurrence matrix. GloVe embeddings are based on global statistics of word co-occurrence frequencies, capturing both local and global semantic relationships between words.

FastText: FastText is an extension of Word2Vec that incorporates subword information by representing words as bags of character n-grams. This enables FastText embeddings to capture morphological and compositional aspects of words, making them more robust to misspellings, inflections, and out-of-vocabulary words.

BERT (Bidirectional Encoder Representations from Transformers): BERT is a state-of-the-art transformer-based model for learning contextual word embeddings by pre-training on large corpora of text data. BERT embeddings capture contextual information from both left and right contexts in a bidirectional manner, enabling models to generate embeddings that are sensitive to the surrounding context.

4. Applications of Word Embeddings

Language Modeling: Word embeddings are used to train language models that predict the next word in a sequence of text, enabling applications such as autocomplete, spelling correction, and text generation.

Text Classification: Word embeddings serve as input features for text classification models, enabling tasks such as sentiment analysis, topic classification, and spam detection.

Information Retrieval: Word embeddings enable semantic search and document retrieval by capturing semantic similarities between words and documents, facilitating more accurate and relevant search results.

Machine Translation: Word embeddings are used in machine translation systems to represent source and target language words, enabling models to learn mappings between words in different languages and generate accurate translations.

Named Entity Recognition (NER): Word embeddings serve as input features for NER models, enabling the identification and classification of named entities such as persons, organizations, and locations in text data.

5. Challenges and Future Directions

Despite their effectiveness, word embeddings have limitations and challenges:

Context Sensitivity: Word embeddings may not capture fine-grained semantic distinctions or context-dependent meanings effectively, leading to ambiguities and inaccuracies in language understanding.

Domain Specificity: Word embeddings trained on generic corpora may not generalize well to specific domains or tasks, requiring domain-specific adaptation or fine-tuning to achieve optimal performance.

Bias and Fairness: Word embeddings may encode biases present in the training data, leading to unintended biases and discriminatory behavior in downstream applications. Addressing bias and fairness concerns in word embeddings requires careful data selection, preprocessing, and algorithmic interventions.

Multilingualism: Word embeddings may not generalize across languages effectively, requiring separate embeddings for different languages or models that capture cross-lingual semantic similarities.

Future directions in word embeddings research include:

Contextualized Embeddings: Developing models that generate contextualized word embeddings sensitive to the surrounding context, enabling more accurate representation of word meanings in different contexts.

Multimodal Embeddings: Integrating information from multiple modalities such as text, images, and audio to generate multimodal embeddings that capture rich semantic relationships across modalities.

Interpretable Embeddings: Designing interpretable embedding models that facilitate human understanding and interpretation of word representations, enabling insights into the semantic structure of word embeddings and their implications for language understanding.

Bias Mitigation: Developing techniques for mitigating biases in word embeddings and promoting fairness and inclusivity in NLP applications, ensuring that word embeddings reflect diverse perspectives and cultural nuances.

word embeddings are a powerful technique for capturing semantic meaning in textual data, enabling a wide range of NLP tasks and applications. By representing words as dense vectors in a continuous vector space, word embeddings facilitate more accurate, efficient, and contextually relevant language understanding. As research in word embeddings continues to advance, addressing challenges such as context sensitivity, bias, and multilingualism, and exploring new directions such as contextualized embeddings and multimodal embeddings, will pave the way for more sophisticated and versatile NLP systems capable of understanding and generating human-like language. Through continued innovation and collaboration, word embeddings will play a central role in unlocking the full potential of natural language understanding and communication in the digital age.

Named Entity Recognition (NER): Extracting Meaningful Entities from Text

Named Entity Recognition (NER) is a fundamental task in natural language processing (NLP) that involves identifying and classifying named entities (NEs) within unstructured text data. Named entities are specific entities that are referred to by proper names, such as persons, organizations, locations, dates, numerical expressions, and other named entities. NER plays a crucial role in various NLP applications, including information extraction, question answering, document summarization, and sentiment analysis. In this detailed exploration, we delve into the concept of Named Entity Recognition, examining its importance, methodologies, challenges, and applications in extracting meaningful entities from text.

1. Introduction to Named Entity Recognition

Named Entity Recognition (NER) is the process of identifying and classifying named entities in text data. Named entities are specific entities that are referred to by proper names, such as persons, organizations, locations, dates, numerical expressions, and other named entities. NER aims to extract and classify these entities into predefined categories or types, enabling machines to understand and analyze the content of text data more effectively.

2. Importance of Named Entity Recognition

NER is essential for several reasons:

Information Extraction: NER plays a crucial role in extracting structured information from unstructured text data, enabling applications such as database population, knowledge graph construction, and semantic annotation.

Semantic Understanding: By identifying and classifying named entities, NER facilitates deeper semantic understanding of text data, enabling machines to discern the meaning, context, and relationships between entities mentioned in the text.

Entity Disambiguation: NER helps disambiguate entities with the same name but different meanings or contexts, enabling more accurate interpretation and analysis of text data.

Document Summarization: NER can be used to identify key entities mentioned in a document, enabling automatic document summarization by highlighting important entities and concepts.

3. Methodologies for Named Entity Recognition

Several methodologies are commonly used for Named Entity Recognition:

Rule-Based Approaches: Rule-based NER systems rely on handcrafted rules and patterns to identify named entities based on linguistic cues such as capitalization, part-of-speech tags, and syntactic patterns. These systems are typically domain-specific and require manual rule creation and maintenance.

Statistical Approaches: Statistical NER systems use machine learning algorithms, such as conditional random fields (CRFs), hidden Markov models (HMMs), or maximum entropy models, to learn patterns and features from annotated training data and predict the labels of named entities in unseen text.

Deep Learning Approaches: Deep learning-based NER systems leverage neural network architectures, such as recurrent neural networks (RNNs), convolutional neural networks (CNNs), or transformer-based models, to learn distributed representations of words and predict the labels of named entities in text data. Models such as Bidirectional Encoder Representations from Transformers (BERT) have achieved state-of-the-art performance in NER tasks by capturing contextual information from large corpora of text data.

4. Challenges in Named Entity Recognition

NER faces several challenges:

Ambiguity: Named entities may have multiple meanings or interpretations, leading to ambiguity in classification. For example, "Apple" could refer to the company Apple Inc. or the fruit.

Variability: Named entities may exhibit variability in terms of spelling, capitalization, and morphology, making it challenging to identify and classify them accurately. For example, "New York" could be written as "NY," "N.Y.," or "New-York."

Out-of-Vocabulary Entities: NER systems may encounter named entities that are not present in the training data or vocabulary, requiring robust mechanisms for handling out-of-vocabulary entities and unknown words.

Domain Adaptation: NER systems may perform differently across different domains or genres of text, requiring domain adaptation techniques to transfer knowledge from one domain to another effectively.

5. Applications of Named Entity Recognition

NER has diverse applications in NLP tasks:

Information Extraction: NER enables the extraction of structured information from unstructured text data, facilitating tasks such as entity linking, relation extraction, and event extraction.

Question Answering: NER helps identify relevant entities mentioned in questions and answers, enabling systems to provide accurate and contextually relevant responses to user queries.

Document Summarization: NER can be used to identify key entities and concepts mentioned in a document, enabling automatic document summarization by highlighting important information.

Sentiment Analysis: NER can help identify entities mentioned in sentiment-bearing text, enabling more fine-grained analysis of opinions, attitudes, and sentiments expressed towards specific entities.

6. Future Directions in Named Entity Recognition

Future directions in NER research include:

Multilingual NER: Developing NER systems that can handle multiple languages and dialects effectively, enabling cross-lingual information extraction and analysis.

Domain-Specific NER: Designing NER systems that are specialized for specific domains or industries, such as biomedical NER for extracting entities from medical texts or financial NER for extracting entities from financial documents.

Zero-shot NER: Exploring zero-shot learning techniques for NER, where models can recognize named entities without explicitly training on annotated data for those entities, enabling more flexible and adaptive NER systems.

Interactive NER: Developing interactive NER systems that can incorporate user feedback and corrections to improve the accuracy and robustness of entity recognition over time.

Named Entity Recognition (NER) is a foundational task in natural language processing (NLP) that plays a crucial role in extracting meaningful entities from unstructured text data. By identifying and classifying named entities such as persons, organizations, locations, and dates, NER enables machines to understand and analyze the content of text data more effectively, facilitating tasks such as information extraction, question answering, document summarization, and sentiment analysis. Despite its challenges, NER continues to be an active area of research, with ongoing efforts to develop more accurate, robust, and versatile NER systems capable of handling diverse languages, domains, and applications. Through continued innovation and collaboration, NER will continue to advance the state-of-the-art in NLP and unlock new possibilities for extracting knowledge and insights from textual data in the digital age.

Sentiment Analysis: Understanding Opinions and Emotions

Sentiment analysis, also known as opinion mining, is a natural language processing (NLP) technique that aims to analyze and interpret the sentiment, opinions, attitudes, and emotions expressed in text data. It involves extracting subjective information from textual content to determine whether the expressed sentiment is positive, negative, or neutral. Sentiment analysis plays a crucial role in various applications, including social media monitoring, customer feedback analysis, brand reputation management, market research, and personalized recommendation systems. In this comprehensive exploration, we delve into the concept of sentiment analysis, examining its importance, methodologies, challenges, and applications in understanding opinions and emotions in text.

1. Introduction to Sentiment Analysis

Sentiment analysis is the process of computationally analyzing and interpreting the sentiment, opinions, attitudes, and emotions expressed in text data. It involves extracting subjective information from textual content to determine the overall sentiment polarity (positive, negative, or neutral) associated with a particular piece of text. Sentiment analysis enables machines to understand and interpret human emotions and opinions expressed in online reviews, social media posts, customer feedback, news articles, and other forms of text data.

2. Importance of Sentiment Analysis

Sentiment analysis is essential for several reasons:

Customer Insights: Sentiment analysis provides valuable insights into customer opinions, preferences, and satisfaction levels, enabling businesses to identify areas for improvement, address customer concerns, and enhance customer experience.

Brand Monitoring: Sentiment analysis helps businesses monitor and manage their brand reputation by tracking mentions of their brand, products, or services on social media, review platforms, and news outlets, enabling proactive reputation management and crisis response.

Market Research: Sentiment analysis enables market researchers to analyze consumer sentiment, identify market trends, and gauge public opinion on products, brands, or topics of interest, providing valuable intelligence for strategic decision-making and product development.

Social Media Analytics: Sentiment analysis is widely used in social media analytics to track sentiment trends, detect emerging topics, and measure the impact of social media campaigns, enabling businesses to optimize their social media strategy and engagement efforts.

3. Methodologies for Sentiment Analysis

Several methodologies are commonly used for sentiment analysis:

Lexicon-Based Approaches: Lexicon-based sentiment analysis relies on predefined dictionaries or lexicons of sentiment-bearing words and their associated sentiment polarity (positive, negative, or neutral). Textual content is analyzed by matching words in the text with entries in the sentiment lexicon and aggregating sentiment scores to determine the overall sentiment polarity

Machine Learning Approaches: Machine learning-based sentiment analysis involves training supervised learning models, such as support vector machines (SVM), Naive Bayes classifiers, or deep learning models, on labeled training data to predict the sentiment polarity of unseen text. Models are trained using features derived from the text, such as word embeddings, n-grams, or syntactic features, and evaluated based on their performance on a held-out test set.

Aspect-Based Sentiment Analysis: Aspect-based sentiment analysis (ABSA) goes beyond overall sentiment polarity to analyze sentiment at a more granular level, focusing on specific aspects or features mentioned in the text (e.g., product features, service attributes). ABSA involves identifying aspect terms and their associated sentiment polarity within the context of opinionated text, enabling more fine-grained analysis of sentiment.

4. Challenges in Sentiment Analysis

Sentiment analysis faces several challenges:

Ambiguity and Subjectivity: Sentiment analysis is inherently subjective and context-dependent, making it challenging to accurately interpret and classify sentiment in text data, especially in cases of sarcasm, irony, or subtle nuances in language.

Language and Cultural Differences: Sentiment analysis models may perform differently across languages and cultures due to variations in linguistic expressions, cultural norms, and idiomatic expressions, requiring language-specific or domain-specific adaptation.

Data Sparsity and Imbalance: Sentiment analysis models may suffer from data sparsity and class imbalance, with insufficient labeled data for underrepresented classes or fine-grained sentiment categories, leading to biased or inaccurate predictions.

Context Sensitivity: Sentiment analysis models may struggle to capture contextual information and long-range dependencies in text data, leading to errors in sentiment classification, especially in cases of complex or ambiguous language.

5. Applications of Sentiment Analysis

Sentiment analysis has diverse applications in various domains:

Brand Monitoring and Reputation Management: Sentiment analysis helps businesses monitor and manage their brand reputation by tracking sentiment trends, identifying positive and negative mentions, and responding to customer feedback in a timely manner.

Customer Feedback Analysis: Sentiment analysis enables businesses to analyze customer feedback, reviews, and survey responses to identify common pain points, sentiment trends, and areas for improvement, enabling data-driven decision-making and customer-centric strategies.

Market Research and Competitive Intelligence: Sentiment analysis provides valuable insights into market trends, consumer preferences, and competitive landscape by analyzing sentiment in product reviews, social media conversations, and industry news, enabling businesses to identify emerging opportunities and threats.

Social Media Monitoring and Crisis Response: Sentiment analysis helps organizations monitor social media conversations, detect potential crises or reputation threats, and respond to negative sentiment in real-time, enabling proactive crisis management and damage control.

6. Future Directions in Sentiment Analysis

Future directions in sentiment analysis research include:

Fine-Grained Sentiment Analysis: Developing models for fine-grained sentiment analysis that can capture nuanced sentiments, emotions, and attitudes expressed in text data, enabling more granular analysis of sentiment categories and sentiment strength.

Multimodal Sentiment Analysis: Integrating information from multiple modalities, such as text, images, and audio, to perform multimodal sentiment analysis that captures sentiment expressed across different modalities and channels, enabling more comprehensive analysis of sentiment in multimedia content.

Cross-Lingual Sentiment Analysis: Developing models for cross-lingual sentiment analysis that can analyze sentiment across multiple languages and cultures, enabling more inclusive and global analysis of sentiment trends and opinions.

Ethical and Fair Sentiment Analysis: Addressing ethical concerns and biases in sentiment analysis models by promoting fairness, transparency, and accountability in data collection, model training, and deployment, ensuring that sentiment analysis systems reflect diverse perspectives and cultural nuances.

Sentiment analysis is a powerful technique for understanding opinions, attitudes, and emotions expressed in text data, with diverse applications across various domains and industries. By analyzing sentiment in textual content, sentiment analysis enables businesses to gain valuable insights into customer opinions, brand reputation, market trends, and social media conversations, facilitating data-driven decision-making and strategic planning. Despite its challenges, sentiment analysis continues to evolve, with ongoing research efforts focused on developing more accurate, robust, and interpretable sentiment analysis models capable of capturing nuanced sentiments, handling cross-lingual and multimodal data, and addressing ethical concerns and biases. Through continued innovation and collaboration, sentiment analysis will remain a cornerstone of NLP research and applications, enabling machines to understand and interpret human emotions and opinions in the digital age.

Chapter 7

Computer Vision: Seeing the World Through Pixels

Computer vision is a field of artificial intelligence (AI) that aims to enable machines to interpret and understand visual information from the world around us. It involves developing algorithms and systems that can analyze and extract meaningful insights from images and videos, mimicking the human ability to perceive and interpret visual stimuli. From object detection and recognition to image segmentation and scene understanding, computer vision plays a crucial role in a wide range of applications, including autonomous vehicles, medical imaging, surveillance, robotics, and augmented reality. In this introduction, we delve into the concept of computer vision, examining its importance, methodologies, challenges, and applications in enabling machines to see and understand the world through pixels.

1. Importance of Computer Vision

Computer vision is essential for several reasons:

Understanding Visual Information: Computer vision enables machines to interpret and understand visual information from images and videos, enabling tasks such as object detection, recognition, and scene understanding.

Automation and Efficiency: Computer vision technology automates visual tasks that were traditionally performed by humans, leading to increased efficiency, productivity, and scalability across various industries and domains.

Insights and Decision-Making: Computer vision provides valuable insights and data-driven decision-making capabilities by analyzing visual data and extracting meaningful patterns, trends, and anomalies from images and videos.

Enabling New Applications: Computer vision drives innovation and enables new applications and technologies, including autonomous vehicles, facial recognition systems, medical imaging devices, and augmented reality experiences, transforming the way we interact with the world around us.

2. Methodologies in Computer Vision

Several methodologies are used in computer vision:

Image Processing: Image processing techniques involve manipulating and enhancing digital images to improve their quality, extract features, or perform specific tasks such as noise reduction, edge detection, and image enhancement.

Feature Extraction and Representation: Feature extraction techniques identify and extract relevant features from images, such as edges, corners, textures, and shapes, to represent visual information in a form suitable for analysis and interpretation.

Machine Learning and Deep Learning: Machine learning and deep learning algorithms, such as convolutional neural networks (CNNs), recurrent neural networks (RNNs), and generative adversarial networks (GANs), are widely used in computer vision tasks to learn patterns and representations directly from visual data, enabling tasks such as image classification, object detection, and image generation.

Geometric and 3D Vision: Geometric and 3D vision techniques involve analyzing the spatial relationships and geometry of objects in images and videos, enabling tasks such as depth estimation, pose estimation, and 3D reconstruction.

3. Challenges in Computer Vision

Computer vision faces several challenges:

Variability and Invariance: Computer vision models must be robust to variations in lighting, viewpoint, scale, occlusion, and background clutter, making it challenging to generalize across diverse visual conditions and environments.

Semantic Understanding: Computer vision models must possess semantic understanding of visual scenes, objects, and concepts, enabling higher-level reasoning and interpretation of visual data beyond pixel-level analysis.

Data Quality and Annotation: Computer vision models require large-scale, annotated datasets for training, which may be costly, time-consuming, and prone to biases, errors, and inaccuracies in data labeling and annotation.

Ethical and Societal Implications: Computer vision technologies raise ethical and societal concerns related to privacy, surveillance, bias, fairness, and accountability, requiring responsible development and deployment practices to address potential risks and unintended consequences.

4. Applications of Computer Vision

Computer vision has diverse applications in various domains:

Autonomous Vehicles: Computer vision enables autonomous vehicles to perceive and interpret their surroundings, detect obstacles, recognize traffic signs, and navigate safely in complex driving environments.

Medical Imaging: Computer vision techniques are used in medical imaging modalities such as X-ray, MRI, and CT scans to assist with diagnosis, treatment planning, and image-guided interventions, enabling early detection and personalized healthcare.

Surveillance and Security: Computer vision systems are used in surveillance cameras and security systems to monitor and analyze video streams, detect suspicious activities or intruders, and enhance public safety and security.

Augmented Reality: Computer vision powers augmented reality (AR) applications that overlay digital information and virtual objects onto the real world, enabling immersive experiences in gaming, entertainment, education, and retail.

5. Future Directions in Computer Vision

Future directions in computer vision research include:

Multimodal Fusion: Integrating information from multiple modalities, such as text, audio, and sensor data, to enhance visual understanding and enable more comprehensive analysis of complex scenes and environments.

Explainable AI: Developing explainable and interpretable computer vision models that can provide insights into their decision-making process, enabling users to understand and trust AI-driven recommendations and predictions.

Robustness and Generalization: Improving the robustness and generalization of computer vision models to variations in data distribution, environmental conditions, and adversarial attacks, enabling more reliable and resilient performance in real-world applications.

Human-Centric Vision: Focusing on human-centric computer vision tasks such as gesture recognition, emotion recognition, and human pose estimation, to enable more natural and intuitive human-computer interaction experiences.

Computer vision is a rapidly evolving field of artificial intelligence that enables machines to interpret and understand visual information from the world around us. By analyzing images and videos, computer vision systems can perform tasks such as object detection, recognition, and scene understanding, with applications ranging from autonomous vehicles and medical imaging to surveillance and augmented reality. Despite its challenges, computer vision continues to advance, with ongoing research efforts focused on developing more robust, interpretable, and ethical computer vision technologies that can empower humans and improve our understanding of the visual world. Through continued innovation and collaboration, computer vision will continue to drive transformative changes across industries and domains, shaping the future of AI-powered visual intelligence.

Image Classification Techniques: A Comprehensive Overview

Image classification is a fundamental task in computer vision that involves categorizing images into predefined classes or categories based on their visual content. It plays a crucial role in various applications, including object recognition, scene understanding, medical diagnosis, and autonomous driving. Over the years, researchers have developed a wide range of techniques and algorithms for image classification, ranging from traditional methods to state-of-the-art deep learning approaches. In this comprehensive overview, we delve into the different image classification techniques, examining their methodologies, strengths, limitations, and applications.

1. Introduction to Image Classification

Image classification is the process of assigning a label or category to an input image based on its visual content. It is one of the foundational tasks in computer vision and serves as the basis for many higher-level vision tasks, such as object detection, segmentation, and recognition. Image classification algorithms analyze the pixel values and features of an image to determine its category, enabling machines to understand and interpret visual information.

2. Traditional Image Classification Techniques

Before the rise of deep learning, traditional image classification techniques relied on handcrafted features and machine learning algorithms:

Feature Extraction: Traditional image classification techniques typically involved extracting low-level features from images, such as color histograms, texture descriptors (e.g., Gabor filters), and local binary patterns (LBP), to represent the visual content of images.

Machine Learning Algorithms: Once features were extracted, machine learning algorithms such as support vector machines (SVM), random forests, and k-nearest neighbors (KNN) were commonly used to train classifiers that could distinguish between different classes of images based on their extracted features.

While traditional techniques were effective to some extent, they often struggled with complex visual patterns and required extensive feature engineering to achieve good performance.

3. Deep Learning-Based Image Classification

Deep learning has revolutionized image classification by enabling end-to-end learning of hierarchical features directly from raw pixel values. Convolutional neural networks (CNNs) have emerged as the dominant architecture for image classification tasks:

Convolutional Neural Networks (CNNs): CNNs are neural network architectures specifically designed for processing grid-structured data, such as images. They consist of multiple layers of convolutional, pooling, and fully connected layers, which learn hierarchical representations of image features from low-level edges and textures to high-level semantic concepts.

Transfer Learning: Transfer learning has become a popular technique for image classification, where pre-trained CNN models (e.g., VGG, ResNet, Inception, and EfficientNet) trained on large-scale datasets such as ImageNet are fine-tuned on smaller, task-specific datasets to adapt them to new classification tasks. This approach leverages the learned representations from pre-trained models and significantly reduces the amount of labeled data required for training.

Data Augmentation: Data augmentation techniques such as random rotations, translations, flips, and scaling are commonly used to artificially increase the diversity of the training data and improve the generalization performance of CNN models, reducing overfitting and improving robustness to variations in input data.

4. Hybrid Approaches

Hybrid approaches combine traditional techniques with deep learning methods to achieve better performance:

Feature Fusion: Feature fusion techniques combine handcrafted features with learned features from deep neural networks to capture complementary information and improve the discriminative power of image classifiers. For example, features extracted from CNNs can be concatenated with handcrafted features or fed into traditional classifiers as additional input features.

Ensemble Learning: Ensemble learning techniques such as bagging, boosting, and stacking combine multiple classifiers to improve classification performance. In image classification, ensembles of CNNs trained with different architectures or initializations can be combined to achieve better generalization and robustness.

5. Evaluation Metrics

Several evaluation metrics are commonly used to assess the performance of image classifiers:

Accuracy: Accuracy measures the proportion of correctly classified images out of the total number of images in the dataset. While accuracy is a widely used metric, it may not be suitable for imbalanced datasets where some classes are more prevalent than others.

Precision and Recall: Precision measures the proportion of true positive predictions out of all positive predictions, while recall measures the proportion of true positive predictions out of all actual positive instances. Precision and recall are useful for evaluating classifier performance in the presence of class imbalance.

F1 Score: The F1 score is the harmonic mean of precision and recall and provides a balanced measure of classifier performance, taking into account both false positives and false negatives.

Confusion Matrix: A confusion matrix is a tabular representation of the true positive, true negative, false positive, and false negative predictions made by a classifier, enabling a more detailed analysis of its performance across different classes.

6. Applications of Image Classification

Image classification has numerous applications across various domains:

Object Recognition: Image classification is used for identifying and categorizing objects within images, enabling applications such as visual search, product recognition, and content-based image retrieval.

Medical Diagnosis: Image classification techniques are employed in medical imaging modalities such as X-ray, MRI, and CT scans to assist with the diagnosis of diseases and abnormalities, such as tumors, fractures, and lesions.

Autonomous Vehicles: Image classification is essential for enabling autonomous vehicles to recognize and classify objects in their environment, such as pedestrians, vehicles, traffic signs, and obstacles, enabling safe navigation and driving decisions.

Biometric Identification: Image classification is used in biometric systems for identifying and verifying individuals based on their facial features, fingerprints, iris patterns, and other biometric traits, enabling applications such as facial recognition and fingerprint authentication.

7. Challenges and Future Directions

Image classification still faces several challenges:

Robustness to Adversarial Attacks: Image classifiers are vulnerable to adversarial attacks, where imperceptible perturbations to input images can cause misclassification. Developing robust image classification models that are resilient to such attacks remains a challenge.

Interpretability and Explainability: Deep learning-based image classifiers often lack interpretability and explainability, making it difficult to understand their decision-making process. Developing methods for interpreting and explaining the predictions of image classifiers is an active area of research.

Generalization to Unseen Domains: Image classifiers trained on one dataset may not generalize well to images from unseen domains or environments. Developing techniques for domain adaptation and transfer learning to improve the generalization performance of image classifiers is an ongoing research direction.

Ethical and Societal Implications: Image classification technologies raise ethical concerns related to privacy, surveillance, bias, fairness, and accountability. Addressing these concerns and ensuring that image classification systems are developed and deployed responsibly is critical for their ethical and equitable use.

Image classification techniques have evolved significantly over the years, from traditional methods relying on handcrafted features to deep learning-based approaches capable of learning hierarchical representations directly from raw pixel values. These techniques have enabled a wide range of applications across various domains, from object recognition and medical diagnosis to autonomous driving and biometric identification. Despite their successes, image classification techniques still face challenges related to robustness, interpretability, generalization, and ethical considerations. Addressing these challenges and advancing the state-of-the-art in image classification will continue to drive innovation and enable new applications in computer vision and beyond.

Object Detection and Localization: An In-depth Exploration

Object detection and localization are fundamental tasks in computer vision that involve identifying and locating objects within images or videos. Unlike image classification, which assigns a single label to an entire image, object detection algorithms detect and localize multiple objects of interest within an image, along with their corresponding bounding boxes. These tasks are crucial for various applications, including autonomous driving, surveillance, augmented reality, and image retrieval. In this detailed exploration, we delve into the concepts of object detection and localization, examining their methodologies, techniques, challenges, and applications.

1. Introduction to Object Detection and Localization

Object detection and localization refer to the processes of identifying and precisely locating objects within images or videos. These tasks are essential for understanding visual scenes and enabling machines to interact with the environment intelligently. Object detection algorithms not only detect the presence of objects but also provide precise localization information in the form of bounding boxes, which specify the spatial extent of each detected object within the image.

2. Object Detection Methodologies

Several methodologies are commonly used for object detection:

Classical Approaches: Classical object detection approaches typically involve two main stages: object proposal generation and object classification. Object proposal methods, such as selective search or edge boxes, generate a set of candidate regions likely to contain objects. Subsequently, these regions are classified using machine learning algorithms, such as support vector machines (SVMs) or convolutional neural networks (CNNs), to determine the presence of objects and their corresponding classes.

Deep Learning Approaches: Deep learning has revolutionized object detection by enabling end-to-end learning of object detectors directly from raw pixel data. Region-based Convolutional Neural Networks (R-CNN), including variants such as Fast R-CNN, Faster R-CNN, and Mask R-CNN, are widely used for object detection tasks. These models first generate region proposals using region proposal networks (RPNs) and then classify and refine the proposals using CNN-based classifiers.

Single Shot Detectors (SSDs): SSDs are one-stage object detection models that simultaneously predict object bounding boxes and class labels for each location in the input image. SSDs achieve real-time performance by eliminating the need for region proposal generation and significantly speeding up the detection process.

YOLO (You Only Look Once): YOLO is another popular one-stage object detection model that divides the input image into a grid and directly predicts bounding boxes and class probabilities for objects within each grid cell. YOLO achieves fast inference speeds and high detection accuracy by jointly optimizing object localization and classification.

3. Object Localization Techniques

Object localization involves precisely determining the spatial extent of objects within images through the localization of their bounding boxes. Several techniques are used for object localization:

Bounding Box Regression: Bounding box regression techniques aim to predict the coordinates of bounding boxes enclosing objects within images. These techniques typically involve training regression models to learn the transformation from initial bounding box coordinates to the coordinates of the ground-truth bounding boxes.

Anchor Boxes: Anchor boxes, also known as default boxes, are predefined bounding boxes of different shapes and sizes that serve as reference templates for object localization. Object detectors use anchor boxes to predict offsets or transformations to match the shapes and sizes of ground-truth objects, enabling accurate localization.

IoU (Intersection over Union) Thresholding: During training, object detection models use the IoU metric to evaluate the overlap between predicted bounding boxes and ground-truth objects. Bounding boxes with IoU values above a certain threshold are considered positive detections, while those with IoU values below the threshold are considered false positives.

4. Challenges in Object Detection and Localization

Object detection and localization face several challenges:

Scale and Aspect Ratio Variability: Objects in images may vary significantly in scale, aspect ratio, and orientation, making it challenging to detect and localize objects accurately across different contexts and viewpoints.

Occlusion and Clutter: Objects may be partially occluded or surrounded by clutter in complex scenes, leading to difficulties in distinguishing objects from background noise and accurately localizing them.

Limited Training Data: Object detection models require large-scale labeled datasets for training, which may be costly and time-consuming to annotate, especially for fine-grained object categories or specialized domains.

Real-time Performance: Many applications, such as autonomous driving and robotics, require object detection algorithms to operate in real-time with low latency and high throughput, posing challenges for achieving a balance between detection accuracy and computational efficiency.

5. Applications of Object Detection and Localization

Object detection and localization have numerous applications across various domains:

Autonomous Driving: Object detection is critical for enabling autonomous vehicles to perceive and understand their surroundings, detect other vehicles, pedestrians, cyclists, and obstacles, and make informed driving decisions.

Surveillance and Security: Object detection plays a vital role in surveillance systems for detecting and tracking suspicious activities, intruders, or unauthorized objects within monitored areas, enhancing public safety and security.

Augmented Reality: Object detection enables augmented reality (AR) applications to detect and overlay virtual objects or information onto the real-world scene captured by a device's camera, creating immersive and interactive experiences.

Medical Imaging: Object detection techniques are used in medical imaging modalities such as X-ray, MRI, and CT scans to assist radiologists with detecting and localizing abnormalities, tumors, lesions, or anatomical structures of interest, aiding in diagnosis and treatment planning.

6. Future Directions in Object Detection and Localization

Future directions in object detection and localization research include:

Efficient Object Detection Models: Developing more efficient object detection models that achieve a balance between detection accuracy and computational efficiency, enabling real-time performance on resource-constrained devices such as smartphones and edge devices.

Domain Adaptation and Few-shot Learning: Investigating domain adaptation and few-shot learning techniques to improve the generalization performance of object detection models across different domains, environments, and datasets with limited labeled data.

Robustness to Adversarial Attacks: Enhancing the robustness of object detection models to adversarial attacks and image perturbations, ensuring that detectors are resilient to malicious manipulation and maintain performance under challenging conditions.

Interpretability and Explainability: Developing methods for interpreting and explaining the predictions of object detection models, enabling users to understand the rationale behind detections and build trust in the reliability of automated systems.

object detection and localization are essential tasks in computer vision that enable machines to understand and interact with the visual world intelligently. These tasks have numerous applications across various domains, from autonomous driving and surveillance to augmented reality and medical imaging. While significant progress has been made in recent years, challenges such as scale variability, occlusion, and real-time performance persist. Addressing these challenges and advancing the state-of-the-art in object detection and localization will continue to drive innovation and enable new applications in computer vision and beyond.

Image Segmentation: Understanding Image Composition

Image segmentation is a fundamental task in computer vision that involves partitioning an image into multiple segments or regions based on the visual content. Unlike object detection, which identifies and localizes specific objects within an image, image segmentation aims to assign a label to each pixel in the image, grouping pixels with similar attributes into coherent regions. Image segmentation plays a crucial role in various applications, including medical image analysis, autonomous driving, satellite imagery analysis, and image editing. In this detailed exploration, we delve into the concepts of image segmentation, examining its methodologies, techniques, challenges, and applications.

1. Introduction to Image Segmentation

Image segmentation is the process of dividing an image into meaningful regions or segments based on the visual properties of the pixels. These segments are typically homogeneous with respect to certain attributes such as color, texture, or intensity, enabling the extraction of semantic information from the image. Image segmentation serves as a fundamental building block for many higher-level computer vision tasks, including object recognition, scene understanding, and image editing.

2. Methodologies for Image Segmentation

Several methodologies are commonly used for image segmentation:

Thresholding: Thresholding is a simple and intuitive segmentation technique that divides an image into foreground and background regions based on a fixed threshold value applied to pixel intensities. Thresholding is effective for segmenting images with well-defined intensity differences between foreground objects and background.

Region-Based Segmentation: Region-based segmentation techniques group pixels into regions based on similarity criteria such as color, texture, or intensity homogeneity. Techniques such as region growing, region splitting and merging, and watershed segmentation are examples of region-based segmentation methods.

Edge-Based Segmentation: Edge-based segmentation methods detect and localize edges or boundaries between different regions in an image. Techniques such as edge detection using gradient-based operators (e.g., Sobel, Prewitt, Canny) or mathematical morphology operations (e.g., dilation, erosion) are commonly used for edge-based segmentation.

Clustering: Clustering-based segmentation techniques cluster pixels into groups based on their feature similarities using clustering algorithms such as k-means clustering or mean shift clustering. Clustering methods are effective for segmenting images with complex distributions of pixel values.

Semantic Segmentation: Semantic segmentation assigns a semantic label to each pixel in an image, classifying pixels into predefined categories such as object classes or scene categories. Deep learning-based approaches, such as fully convolutional networks (FCNs) and U-Net architectures, have achieved state-of-the-art performance in semantic segmentation tasks.

3. Techniques for Image Segmentation

Various techniques and algorithms are used to perform image segmentation:

Pixel-Based Segmentation: Pixel-based segmentation techniques assign a label to each pixel in the image based on its visual properties, such as color, texture, or intensity. These techniques often involve clustering or thresholding operations to group pixels with similar attributes into coherent regions.

Region-Based Segmentation: Region-based segmentation techniques divide an image into regions or segments based on homogeneity criteria, such as color similarity or intensity consistency. These techniques typically involve iterative region growing or splitting and merging processes to refine the segmentation results.

Boundary-Based Segmentation: Boundary-based segmentation techniques detect and localize boundaries or edges between different regions in the image. Edge detection algorithms, such as the Canny edge detector or the Sobel operator, are commonly used to identify discontinuities in pixel intensities and delineate object boundaries.

Contour-Based Segmentation: Contour-based segmentation techniques extract object contours or outlines from the image and use them as the basis for segmentation. Contour detection algorithms, such as the active contours (snakes) or the Hough transform, are used to identify and extract object boundaries.

Deep Learning-Based Segmentation: Deep learning-based segmentation methods leverage convolutional neural networks

(CNNs) to learn hierarchical representations of image features and perform pixel-wise classification or regression tasks. Fully convolutional networks (FCNs), U-Net architectures, and deep labelling models are popular choices for semantic segmentation tasks.

4. Challenges in Image Segmentation

Image segmentation faces several challenges:

Ambiguity and Variability: Images may contain regions with similar visual properties or ambiguous boundaries, making it challenging to accurately segment objects or regions of interest.

Complexity and Texture: Images with complex textures, cluttered backgrounds, or intricate patterns pose challenges for segmentation algorithms, as they may struggle to distinguish between foreground and background regions.

Noise and Artifacts: Image segmentation algorithms are sensitive to noise, artifacts, and inconsistencies in the image data, which can degrade segmentation accuracy and introduce errors into the segmentation results.

Computational Complexity: Some segmentation algorithms, especially deep learning-based approaches, may require significant computational resources and memory, limiting their applicability in real-time or resource-constrained environments.

5. Applications of Image Segmentation

Image segmentation has numerous applications across various domains:

Medical Image Analysis: Image segmentation is used in medical imaging modalities such as MRI, CT, and ultrasound to segment anatomical structures, tumors, lesions, or abnormalities, enabling diagnosis, treatment planning, and image-guided interventions.

Autonomous Driving: Image segmentation is essential for enabling autonomous vehicles to perceive and understand their surroundings, segmenting road scenes into drivable areas, lanes, vehicles, pedestrians, and obstacles, enabling safe navigation and driving decisions.

Satellite Imagery Analysis: Image segmentation is used in satellite imagery analysis for land cover classification, urban planning, environmental monitoring, and disaster response, enabling the extraction of valuable information from remote sensing data.

Object Detection and Recognition: Image segmentation serves as a preprocessing step for object detection and recognition tasks, providing segmentation masks or regions of interest for identifying and localizing objects within images.

6. Future Directions in Image Segmentation

Future directions in image segmentation research include:

Developing weakly supervised and unsupervised learning techniques for image segmentation that require less annotated data and can learn from weak or noisy supervision signals.

Spatio-Temporal Segmentation: Extending image segmentation methods to spatio-temporal data such as videos, enabling the segmentation of dynamic scenes and the tracking of objects over time.

Interactive and Attention-Based Segmentation: Integrating interactive or attention-based mechanisms into segmentation models to allow users to provide feedback or guidance during the segmentation process, improving the accuracy and interpretability of segmentation results.

Robustness and Generalization: Improving the robustness and generalization performance of segmentation algorithms to variations in input data, environmental conditions, and imaging modalities, ensuring reliable performance across diverse scenarios.

Image segmentation is a fundamental task in computer vision that plays a crucial role in various applications, from medical imaging and autonomous driving to satellite imagery analysis and object recognition. Despite its challenges, image segmentation techniques have evolved significantly over the years, from traditional methods based on pixel clustering to deep learning-based approaches capable of learning complex image representations. Addressing the challenges and advancing the state-of-the-art in image segmentation will continue to drive innovation and enable new applications in computer vision and beyond. Through ongoing research and development efforts, image segmentation will remain a cornerstone of visual perception and understanding in artificial intelligence.

Face Recognition and Biometrics: Enhancing Identity Verification

Face recognition is a biometric technology that enables the identification or verification of individuals based on their facial features. It has gained significant attention and adoption due to its non-intrusive nature, ease of use, and potential applications in various domains, including security, surveillance, access control, and authentication systems. In this comprehensive exploration, we delve into the concepts of face recognition and biometrics, examining their methodologies, techniques, challenges, and applications.

1. Introduction to Face Recognition and Biometrics

Biometrics refers to the measurement and analysis of unique biological or behavioral characteristics of individuals for identification or verification purposes. Face recognition is a biometric modality that relies on capturing and analyzing facial features to determine a person's identity. It involves capturing an image or video of a person's face, extracting distinctive facial features or patterns, and comparing them against a database of enrolled faces to identify or verify the person's identity.

2. Methodologies for Face Recognition

Several methodologies are commonly used for face recognition:

Feature-Based Methods: Feature-based face recognition methods extract distinctive features or landmarks from facial images, such as key points, edges, or textures, and use them to represent and match faces. Techniques such as Eigenfaces, Fisherfaces, and Local Binary Patterns (LBP) are examples of feature-based methods.

Appearance-Based Methods: Appearance-based face recognition methods capture and compare the overall appearance or representation of facial images using techniques such as template matching, correlation-based matching, or deep learning-based approaches. Convolutional Neural Networks (CNNs) and Siamese networks are examples of appearance-based methods.

3D Face Recognition: 3D face recognition methods capture and analyze the three-dimensional geometry or shape of facial surfaces to identify or verify individuals. Techniques such as 3D morphable models, depth sensors, and structured light scanners are used to acquire and analyze 3D facial data.

Deep Learning-Based Methods: Deep learning-based face recognition methods leverage convolutional neural networks (CNNs) to learn hierarchical representations of facial features directly from raw pixel data. Deep learning models such as FaceNet, VGGFace, and ArcFace have achieved state-of-the-art performance in face recognition tasks.

3. Techniques for Face Recognition

Various techniques and algorithms are used to perform face recognition:

Face Detection: Face detection is the process of locating and localizing faces within images or video frames. Techniques such as Viola-Jones, Histogram of Oriented Gradients (HOG), and deep learning-based object detection methods (e.g., SSD, Faster R-CNN) are commonly used for face detection.

Face Alignment: Face alignment techniques preprocess facial images by aligning facial landmarks or fiducial points to a canonical pose or configuration, improving the accuracy and robustness of subsequent face recognition algorithms.

Feature Extraction: Feature extraction techniques extract discriminative features or representations from facial images, such as Eigenfaces, Histogram of Oriented Gradients (HOG), Local Binary Patterns (LBP), or deep learning-based feature descriptors learned from CNNs.

Matching and Classification: Matching and classification algorithms compare the extracted features or representations of the input face against a database of enrolled faces to identify or verify the person's identity. Techniques such as nearest neighbor search, cosine similarity, or softmax classification are commonly used for matching and classification.

4. Challenges in Face Recognition and Biometrics

Face recognition and biometrics face several challenges:

Variability in Facial Appearance: Facial appearance may vary due to changes in lighting conditions, facial expressions, occlusions (e.g., glasses, hats), and aging, making it challenging to accurately recognize faces under diverse conditions.

Privacy and Ethical Concerns: Face recognition technologies raise privacy concerns related to the collection, storage, and use of biometric data, as well as potential misuse or abuse of facial recognition systems for surveillance, tracking, or profiling purposes.

Robustness to Adversarial Attacks: Face recognition systems are vulnerable to adversarial attacks, where imperceptible perturbations to facial images can lead to misclassification or unauthorized access. Developing robust and resilient face recognition algorithms to adversarial manipulation is an ongoing challenge.

Bias and Fairness: Face recognition systems may exhibit biases or disparities in performance across demographic groups (e.g., race, gender), leading to unfair or discriminatory outcomes. Ensuring fairness, transparency, and accountability in face recognition algorithms is essential to mitigate bias and promote equitable deployment.

5. Applications of Face Recognition and Biometrics

Face recognition and biometrics have numerous applications across various domains:

Security and Surveillance: Face recognition is used in security and surveillance systems for access control, identity verification, and monitoring purposes, enabling the detection and recognition of individuals in real-time video streams or surveillance footage.

Biometric Authentication: Face recognition is used for biometric authentication in mobile devices, computers, and online services, enabling users to unlock devices, access accounts, and authorize transactions using their facial features.

Law Enforcement and Forensics: Face recognition is used by law enforcement agencies for criminal identification, suspect tracking, and forensic analysis, enabling the matching of faces against databases of known criminals or suspects.

Border Control and Immigration: Face recognition is used in border control and immigration systems for passport verification, visa processing, and border security, enabling the automated inspection and verification of travelers' identities at border checkpoints.

6. Future Directions in Face Recognition and Biometrics

Future directions in face recognition and biometrics research include:

Privacy-Preserving Techniques: Developing privacy-preserving face recognition techniques that protect individuals' biometric data and ensure user privacy while enabling secure and accurate identity verification.

Multimodal Biometrics: Integrating multiple biometric modalities (e.g., face, fingerprint, iris) for more robust and accurate identity verification, reducing reliance on any single biometric modality and improving recognition performance.

Ethical and Regulatory Frameworks: Establishing ethical guidelines, standards, and regulatory frameworks for the responsible development and deployment of face recognition technologies, ensuring transparency, fairness, and accountability in their use.

Continual Learning and Adaptation: Developing face recognition systems capable of continual learning and adaptation to changing environmental conditions, new faces, and evolving threats, ensuring long-term reliability and effectiveness in real-world applications.

Face recognition is a biometric technology that enables the identification or verification of individuals based on their facial features. It has gained widespread adoption and applications in various domains, including security, surveillance, access control, and authentication systems. Despite its challenges, face recognition continues to evolve, driven by advancements in deep learning, computer vision, and biometric technologies. Addressing the challenges and advancing the state-of-the-art in face recognition and biometrics will continue to drive innovation and enable new applications in identity verification and authentication. Through responsible development and deployment practices, face recognition technologies have the potential to enhance security, convenience, and accessibility in a wide range of applications while respecting user privacy and ethical considerations.

www.ingramcontent.com/pod-product-compliance
Lightning Source LLC
LaVergne TN
LVHW061550070526
838199LV00077B/6987